ISBN 978-0-265-95639-7
PIBN 10915326

This book is a reproduction of an important historical work. Forgotten Books uses
state-of-the-art technology to digitally reconstruct the work, preserving the original format
whilst repairing imperfections present in the aged copy. In rare cases, an imperfection in
the original, such as a blemish or missing page, may be replicated in our edition. We do,
however, repair the vast majority of imperfections successfully; any imperfections that
remain are intentionally left to preserve the state of such historical works.

CATALOGUE

OF

AMERICAN AND FOREIGN COINS,

In Gold, Silver and Copper,

TO BE SOLD WITHOUT RESERVE.

Messrs. BANGS & CO., Auctioneers,

739 and 741 Broadway,

NEW YORK.

This Catalogue is forwarded to Collectors with t

Compliments of

who will be pleased to execute any orders.

Purchasers will oblige those to whom their ord

4 pp 1101 lots

priced

crowns, Syr.
cadrachm passed @
25, mostly misc.
-S.

.OGUE

ND FOREIGN

and Copper

MEDALS,

ier Valuable Pieces,

AND HALF-DOLLAR. LARGEST
K AND LUNEBERG "WILD
SOLD IN AMERICA.

DECORATIONS; FINE ASSORT-
ONEY; FOREIGN CROWNS;
EDALLION; POSTAGE
CATALOGUES,
S, &c.,

C

AT AUCTION,

BY

Messrs. BANGS & CO.,

Nos. 739 and 741 Broadway, New York,

Thursday and Friday, Feb. 12th and 13th,

COMMENCING AT **2** O'CLOCK P. M.

The Coins will be on Exhibition each day, from 9 A. M. until 1.30 P. M.

Gentlemen unable to attend the Sale can have their orders faithfully executed
by the Auctioneers and by Dealers in Coins and Curiosities.

Catalogued by H. G. SAMPSON, cor. Broadway and Fulton St., N. Y.

(Residence, 91 BUSHWICK AVENUE, BROOKLYN, E. D.)

1885.

CATALOGUE

OF

AMERICAN AND FOREIGN

Gold, Silver and Copper

COINS AND MEDALS,

Including, among other Valuable Pieces,

VARITIES OF THE 1795 DOLLAR AND HALF-DOLLAR. LARGEST ASSORTMENT OF BRUNSWICK AND LUNEBERG "WILD MAN" CROWNS EVER SOLD IN AMERICA.

WAR MEDALS, CROSSES AND DECORATIONS; FINE ASSORT- MENT OF CONFEDERATE MONEY; FOREIGN CROWNS; GENUINE SYRACUSE MEDALLION; POSTAGE STAMPS, COIN CATALOGUES, CABINETS, &c.,

TO BE SOLD AT AUCTION,

BY

Messrs. BANGS & CO.,

Nos. 739 and 741 Broadway, New York,

Thursday and Friday, Feb. 12th and 13th,

COMMENCING AT **2** o'CLOCK P. M.

The Coins will be on Exhibition each day, from 9 A. M. until 1.30 P. M.

Gentlemen unable to attend the Sale can have their orders faithfully executed by the Auctioneers and by Dealers in Coins and Curiosities.

Catalogued by H. G. SAMPSON, cor. Broadway and Fulton St., N. Y.

(Residence, 91 BUSHWICK AVENUE, BROOKLYN, E. D.)

1885.

CATALOGUE.

MISCELLANEOUS.

2. 1 Hard Times Tokens. Webster, Credit, Currency, &c. 16 pcs

5￢ 2 Colonials. New Jersey, Connecticut, Fugio, and two others. Nearly poor   5 pcs

10 3 Denarii of Philip I., Gordianus III., Etruscilla, and three others. Ordinary   6 pcs

8 4 Counterfeits of Ancient Denarii (5) and Greek Drachmas, &c.   9 pcs

2. 5 Copy of a Jewish Shekel. Lead. Fine

2 6 Medals of Robert Fulton, Gen. Geary, D. M. Lyle and Thos. Wildey. Size 20 to 24   4 pcs

7 7 Continental Currency, 1776. W. m. proof. A few slight nicks on edge

5 8 Geo. Washington. Head to r.; rev. Edward Cogan's Card. W. m. Fine   Size 20

6 9 Luther. Bust; rev. "7th Jubilee of the Great Reformation," etc., 1867. W. m. proof   Size 25

6 10 Edward Everett. Head; rev. Head of John Bell, and head of Everett; rev. "Boston, July 4th, 1860." Oration by Everett. Fine. Size 20   2 pcs

3 11 Political Medals of Buckalew and Hartranft in c., br., and w. m. Fine. Size 18   4 pcs

2 12 Henry Bogert. Sage's Num. Gal. No. 2, and one of Maj. Gen. Berry. Cop. Size 18x20   2 pcs

2 3/4 13 Japan. Large oval copper coins, square holes in centres. Very good. Size 20x32   75 pcs

1 14 Norway. 5 Ore. Various kings and dates. Many varieties. Ordinary   584 pcs

15 Norway. 5 Ore. Another lot. Varieties   566 pcs

16 Norway. 5 Ore. Another lot   187 pcs

17 Norway. 2 and 1 Ore. Various French, Dutch, Italian, and other foreign coppers   493 pcs

18 Norway. 2 Ore and 1 Ore. Various French, Austrian, Dutch, and other foreign coppers. Good   592 pcs

19 Norway. 2 and 1 Ore, etc. Good   301 pcs

20 Germany. 2 and 1 Reich-pfennings. Many varieties. Ordinary   472 pcs

21 Netherlands. 1 Cent. Many dates and varieties. Good lot   207 pcs

22 Sweden. 5 Ore. Varieties   61 pcs

23 Sweden. 1 Ore. Varieties. Fine   80 pcs

24 Turkey. Coppers. Half-penny size. Good   8 pcs

25 China. Cash. Many varieties and sizes. Ordinary. 226 pcs

26 Austria. 4 Kreutzers. Varieties   49 pcs

27 France. Dix Centimes. Varieties. Ordinary   30 pcs

28 England. Pennies. Various dates and varieties   80 pcs *poor*

29 England. Another lot   99 pcs ″

30 Miscellaneous Foreign Coppers, mostly farthing size. Ordinary   207 pcs

31 Foreign Coppers, mostly French, half-penny size   140 pcs

lot 35 32 Selected lot of Coppers, many have been artistically flattened on a car-track, others have holes in them, and others are simply dampoor   150 pcs

33 Ancient Roman. Small brass. Various Emperors. Poor *Very poor*   54 pcs

34 Washington Cent, 1791; Sovereign of Victoria, etc. Lead   12 pcs

35 German Base Silver Coins, most 5 pfennings. Good. 850 pcs

36 Swedish Base Silver Coins. 10 Ore. Good   52 pcs

37 1793 Cent. Chain poor, but date plain. Scarce

38 Lot of Cents, from 1798 to 1857. Good. 24 pierced   262 pcs

39 Feuchtwanger Cent; English drachm weight. Siege Quarter-Crown, &c. Interesting lot   10 pcs

40 1794 Half-Dime. A very skillfully executed counterfeit, struck in lead

41 Counterfeit Dollars (4), half do. (6), quarters (3), and 5 Franc piece of Louis Phillippe, struck in lead   14 pcs

15 42 Quarter-Dollar of 1820 and Spanish Sixpence, pierced (both poor), and pattern 2½ gold pieces of 1843 and 1861. 4 pcs

2 6 43 1796 Half-Cent. Broken die. Calculated to deceive. Very good and desirable. Electrotype

13 44 Half-Cents. 1840, 1, 3, 4, 5 and 6. Very fine. Electrotype 6 pcs

6 45 Half-Cents. 1795, 7 (2), and others, one pierced, and 2 Cents 1872 (2) 12 pcs

1 46 Cents. 1879 (3), 80 (3), 82 (5) and 83. Uncirculated. Red 29 pcs

5 47 Five Cents Nickel. 1883. Uncirculated 5 pcs

130 48 Dollar. 1797. Very fair. Scarce

130 49 Dollar. 1797. Very fair. Scarce

120 50 Dollar. 1798. Ordinary

100 51 Dollar. 1850. Deep scratch in field, otherwise good

170 52 Dollar. 1856. Fine. Scarce.

50 53 Half-Dollar. 1806 and 1814. Ordinary 2 pcs

25 54 Quarter-Dollar. 1815. Good for date. Scarce

14 55 Twenty Cent, 1876. Dimes of 1805 and 11. Ordinary and poor 3 pcs

40 56 Dime. 1846. Very fair. Scarce

14 57 Half-Dime, 1795, pierced ; 1800 (2), 1838 (O mint) and 1856; and 1855, 57 and 66 3-Cent Silver piece. Good 8 pcs

27 58 Geo. III. 3d. 1762. A little gem, rare in this condition

11 59 Brazil Quarter-Dollar and Danish W. I. 5 Cent. Good 2 pcs

2/8 60 Confederate Money; 50c., $1, 2, 5 (6 varieties), 10 (6 varieties), 20 (4 varieties), 50 and 100 (2). Fine condition 23 pcs

4 61 Continental Notes. Pennsylvania 4d., 6d., 1s. (2), 18d., 2s., 6s., 8s. Good 8 pcs

9 62 Intaglios. Bird on spray, dog and bird, rooster, lion, Fortune, and 3 crests. In carnelian, chalcedony, bloodstone, and amethyst. Good lot 8 pcs

1½ 63 Coin Catalogues. Scott & Co. *One priced* 19 pcs

½ 64 Coin Catalogues. W. E. Woodward. *Eight priced* 28 pcs

65 Coin Catalogues. H. P. Smith. *Four priced* 16 pcs

¼ 66 Coin Catalogues. Edw. & Geo. Cogan. *One priced* 11 pcs

67 Coin Catalogues. J. W. Hasletine. *Four priced* 26 pcs

68 Coin Catalogues. S. K. Harzfeld. *Two priced* 6 pcs

1 69 Coin Catalogues. H. G. Sampson. *One priced* 11 pcs
1/4 70 Coin Catalogues. Edw. Frossard. *Eight priced* 35 pcs
1/4 71 Coin Catalogues. Chapman Bros. *Five priced* 12 pcs
55 72 Coin Catalogue. Coll. of Chas J. Bushnell. *Priced* Scarce
1/4 73 Coin Catalogues. Miscellaneous. *Four priced* 22 pcs
2 5 74 Anthon Cabinet. Parts 1, 2, 3 and 4 4 pcs
2 3/4 75 Coin Collectors' Journal. Various numbers 25 pcs

FOREIGN COPPER COINS.

19 76 Morocco. Star; rev. various dates. Good . 6 pcs
19 77 Morocco. Same. Varieties 6 pcs
4 78 England. Druid Head Penny, 1787. Southampton, Edinburgh, Bristol and other Half-Pennies. Gool lot 9 pcs
1/2 79 England. Penny Tokens of New Brunswick, Nova Scotia, Canada, etc. Good 11 pcs
1 80 England. Farthings of George III (2); Quarter Annas of the E. I. Co. (3), and two others. Good 7 pcs
18 81 Bermuda and St. Helena Half-Pennies. Ordinary 2 pcs
15 82 Coventry Half-Penny, 1793. Lady Godiva naked. Fair
2 83 Denmark, Sweden and Norway. Coppers of Charles XV., Oscar, Fred. VI. Various dates and denominations. Good 7 pcs
2 84 Denmark. 1 (2), ½ and ⅛ Skilling. Good 4 pcs
2 85 Sicily. Ferd. III., 1815; Francis I., 1825, and 30 Kreutzer of Austria, penny size. And Soldi of Italy, 1813. Fair 4 pcs
2 86 France, 1853. Dix-Centimes of Napoleon III., and Penny and Half-Penny of Victoria, 1861 and 2. Uncirculated. Red 3 pcs
8 87 Isle of Man Half-Penny and Farthing, 1839. Good 2 pcs
4 88 Denmark. 1 Or, 1736, 46, 7, 51, and ½ Skilling, 1803. Ordinary 5 pcs
2 1/2 89 Russia. 5, 2 (10), 1 (3) and 1 Lepta. Various dates. Good 15 pcs
1 1/2 90 Lot of Coppers, from farthing to penny size, of England, France, Russia, Turkey, Sicily, Portugal, Denmark, etc., etc. Good lot 145 pcs
1/2 91 Germany. 2 Pfenning. Various dates. Ordinary 75 pcs

/2 92 Turkey.   Dollar size.   Base silver

3 93 Medals of Victoria, New Royal Ex., London, and Garibaldi.
W. M.   Size 28   3 pcs

55 94 Greenland.   1863.   A. Gibbs & Son.   "Ost Granland 1
Daler."   Brass.   Very good   Size 22

3 95 Base Silver Coins of Spain, Germany, Sweden, Switzerland,
South America, Belgium, France, etc.   1 pierced, from 5c.
to 20c. size   45 pcs

9 96 Hayti.   Base Silver.   Dollar, half, quarter and dime of
Petion and Boyer.   Ordinary   4 pcs

SILVER COINS.

52/2 97 Ancient.   Caracalla, *Brit.* type ;   and Trajanus Decius,
Denarii.   Good   2 pcs

/8 98 Ancient.   Philip I (The Arabian) Varieties.   Denarii.   Good
6 pcs

/0 99 Ancient.   Gordianus III (2) and Otacilia.   Ordinary.   3 pcs

/6 100 Ancient.   Dyrrachium and Macedon, Drachms and 2 Family
Coins.   Pierced   4 pcs

// 101 Ancient   Dyrrachium Drachm and two Family Denarii, one
with loop.   Poor   3 pcs

6½ 102 Ancient.   Denarii of Vespasian Augustus, Trajan, Hadrian,
Faustina, etc.   Poor and pierced   14 pcs

55 103 Ancient.   Silvered Electrotype.   Helmeted head "Alexan-
dros;"   rev. Alexander, with a captive in a triumphal car,
drawn by four elephants.   With ring and loop.   Size 23

/40 104 Austria.   1603.   Figure of the Emperor with sword, &c.;
rev. Horseman within a circle of 15 shields.   Very good.
Crown

75 105 Poland.   1701.   Fred. August.   Bust.   Rev. Double shield
of arms crowned.   ⅔ Crown.   Very good

87 106 Denmark.   1723.   Frederick III.   King on horseback;   rev.
Arms.   4 Marks Dansk.   Crown size *Partially pierced poor*

/86 107 England.   George I.   1723.   Crown.   S. S. C.   South Sea
Company.   Good

95 108 Austria.   1780.   Maria Theresa.   Bust.   Rev. Arms.   Crown.
Very fine and sharp

75 109 Prussia.   1785.   Frederick the Great.   Thaler.   Good

8 5 110 Spain. 1815. Charles VII. Pillar Dollar. Very fine
1 1 6 111 France. Medal of the Royal Conservatory. Laureated
head of Louis Philippe to r.; rev. Inscription engraved
within a fine olive wreath. By *Caqué.* Proof. Size 26
9 0 112 France. 1868. Napoleon III. 5 Francs. Fine
9 0 113 France. 1873. 5 Francs of the Republic. Uncirculated.
A slight scratch in field
4 0 114 Bolivia. 1863. Medal Half-Dollar. Busts of Melgarejo
and Munoz jugata; rev. Inscription. Good
1 0 115 Sardinia. Vict. Amed. 1796. 20 Soldi.—Denmark. Frederick. 1716. 16 Skilling and ⅙ Daler. Good. Size 17
3 pcs
5 0 116 England. 1787. Geo. III. ~~Pattern~~ Shilling. Uncirculated
1 0 117 England. Anna. Farthing. Silvered Electrotype. Size 15
2 6 118 Japan Itzebue and ¼ Itzabue. Fine   2 pcs
4 ½ 119 Mexico. Maximilian Dime and 5 Cent. Peru, France, Hong
Kong, Prussia, Norway and Siam. 2 pierced. Silver
value 70 cents   12 pcs

AMERICAN SILVER.

1 1 5 120 Dollar. 1795. Flowing hair. Good
1 1 5 121 Dollar. 1795. Fillet head. Ordinary
1 4 5 122 Dollar. 1796. Ordinary
1 5 5 123 Dollar. 1797. Very fair. Scarce
1 1 5 124 Dollar. 1798. Good
1 2 0 125 Dollar. 1800. Good
1 4 0 126 Dollar. 1801. Good
1 3 0 127 Dollar. 1802. Good
1 4 0 128 Dollar. 1803. Good
1 1 6 129 Dollar. 1870. Nicked proof
1 0 5 130 Dollar. 1871. Slightly injured. Proof
1 0 5 131 Dollar. 1873. Slightly injured. Proof
6 5 132 Half-Dollar. 1795. Good
6 0 133 Half-Dollar. 1803. Good
5 0 134 Half-Dollar. 1805. Very fair
5 0 135 Half-Dollar. 1806. Blunt 6. Good
5 5 136 Half-Dollar. 1809. Uncirculated
9 0 137 Half-Dollar. 1814. Uncirculated

Half-Dollar. 1815. Very good. Obv. scratched. Scarce
Half-Dollar. 1851. Good
Half-Dollar. 1852. O. Mint. Good. Scarce
Quarter-Dollar. 1796. Obv. very fair; rev. poor. Scarce
Quarter-Dollar. 1804. Very fair. Scarce
Dime. 1796. Obv. fair; rev. poor. Scarce
Dime. 1846. Good. Scarce
Dime. 1846. Good. Scarce
Half-Dime. 1795. Good. Scarce
Half-Dime. 1800. Good for date. Scarce
Half-Dime. 1829. Very fine
Half-Dime. 1831. Proof
Half-Dime. 1831, 2, 3, 4. Very good 4 pcs
Half-Dime. 1835 and 1837. Starless. Uncirculated 2 pcs
Half-Dime. 1837. With and without stars, and '38 with-
out stars. O Mint. Good and very good 3 pcs
Half-Dime. 1839, 40, 1, 3. Uncirculated 4 pcs
Half-Dime. 1844. Fine
Half-Dime. 1844. O Mint. Very good
Half-Dime. 1849, 53, 7, 9. Very fine, only a trifle touched
by friction 4 pcs
Half-Dime. 1862, 68. S. Mint. Fine 2 pcs
Half-Dime. 1873. Proof
Three Cents. 1851. Uncirculated
Three Cents. 1853. Uncirculated
Three Cents. 1854. Uncirculated
Three Cents. 1855. Good
Three Cents. 1859. Uncirculated 2 pcs
Three Cents. 1861, 2. Very good 2 pcs
Three Cents. 1867. Brilliant proof
Three Cents. 1870. Brilliant proof
Three Cents. 1871. Brilliant proof
Three Cents. 1872. Brilliant proof
Three Cents. 1872. Proof
Three Cents. 1872. Proof
Three Cents. 1873. Brilliant proof. Rare
Medal. Geo. Washington. Head; rev., "Time increases
his fame." Tarnished proof. Size 18

CENTS, PAPER MONEY, AND CURIOSITIES.

30 173 Cents. 1818, 20, 50. Uncirculated. Red   3 pcs

30 174 Cents. 1818, 20, 53. Uncirculated. Red   3 pcs

34 175 Cents. 1818, 20, 56. Uncirculated. Red   3 pcs

2¼ 176 Cents. 1794 to 1857. Poor and fair   59 pcs

2 177 Cents. 1857, 8, 9, 60, 62, 63 nickel, and 1864, 79, 80, 2, 3, copper. Uncirculated   11 pcs

7 178 Colonials. Conn. (2), Mass. Fugio, N. H. Token, and another. Barely fair   6 pcs

2½ 179 Hard Times Tokens. Various, and " Am I not a Woman and a Sister ?" Ordinary   11 pcs

1 180 Store Card. W. A. Brown & Co. Brass (5) and w. m. Fine   9 pcs

1 181 Store Card. N. G. Folger. Brass (5) and copper. Uncirculated   10 pcs

1 182 Store Card. R. Lovett, Jr. Brass (10) and copper. Uncirculated   15 pcs

11 183 Hard Times Token. 1837. Tortoise and safe; rev. Jackass running. Uncirculated. Red   3 pcs

1 184 Medal of G. Washington, rev. blank, w. m.; and one of G. B. McClellan, rev. blank, brass. Good. Size 19   2 pcs

½ 185 Copperheads. A variety. Ordinary   50 pcs

2¼ 186 Wildcat Bank Bills. $5 (15), $2 (15) and $1. Good   50 pcs

1⅛ 187 " Absolute Money." $100. With portraits of Ben. Butler and Dennis Kearney. *Uncirculated*   25 pcs

1 188 Confederate Money. $100 (5), $10 (12), $5 (8). Fine   25 pcs

1 189 War Envelopes. Many of the illus. colored. Good lot   50 pcs

¾ 190 Postage Stamps. A miscellaneous lot of foreign and American. All genuine   600 pcs

1¼ 191 Confederate Postage. 10 (30) and 20 cents   55 pcs

1¾ 192 Foreign and American Proprietary and Express Stamps. A great variety. Unused   165 pcs

½ 193 U. S. Revenue. Postage and official, and a few foreign   505 pcs

55 194 Chinese ~~Ivory~~ *Bone* Carving. Woman and vase. Suitable for a knife handle. Length 4½ in.

Bone

$\int \int \bar{1}$95 Chinese ~~Ivory~~ Carving. Monkey on a tree. Similar. Length 5½ in.

22-196 Section of the Original Atlantic Cable. Length 4 in.

$\int o$ {197 Terra-Cotta Gourd. Antique. Length 2½ in.

{198 Terra-Cotta Vase, flaring mouth. Light terra-cotta from Cyprus. Height 4½ in.

ANCIENT JAPANESE TEMPLE MONEY.

$8 \int \bar{1}$99 Shinto or temple money, shaped like a wheel with 8 spokes. A man leading a horse on obv. Very good   Size 31

$\int \int \bar{2}$00 Kanya, 1623. A thick "Cash" encircled by two branches, forming a wreath, with handle. Fine. Rare. Size 34x44   "

$42 \int \bar{2}$01 Komahiki. Very similar to last, without loop. Fine. Rare   Size 32x30   //

$/0 \int \bar{2}$02 Sen-dai-tsu-ho. Nearly square, with rounded corners, the square hole in centre surrounded by characters on obv.; on rev. two rows to r. and l. Very fine   Size 45   //

$\int \sigma \sigma$203 Very large, round Medal. Characters on obv. and rev. Very fine and very rare   Size 83 or 5⅛ in. diam.   _.

$/0 \int \bar{2}$04 Temple Medal Coin, heart-shaped. No hole in centre, but the field on either side of centre removed. Very curious. Rare   Size 30x39   //

70 205 Temple Cash. Two Cash joined and fastened to support. Very curious   Size 29x33   //

$//0$ 206 Temple Cash. Fork shaped, the hole at the top. Very curious.   Size 64x23   //

$/ \int \tau$ 207 Temple Cash. Razor shaped. Very fine. "Tserh—merh—taow," State of *Tse.*   Size 112 or 7 in. by 20   //

$\int \tau$ 208 California Gold Half-Dollar. A miner digging gold; rev. "H. Cal. gold charm." Octagonal. Proof

$3 \int \bar{2}$09 California Gold Half-Dollar. Same

$3 \int \bar{2}$10 Same. Round and octagonal   2 pcs

$4 \int \bar{2}$11 Same. Round and octagonal   2 pcs

$3 /$ 212 Similar. Round   2 pcs

$\int /$ 213 Similar. Round   2 pcs

WAR MEDALS.

Unless otherwise mentioned, all have ribbons.

30 214 AUSTRIA. Maltese Cross encircled by wreath. "Europe's liberty maintained, 1813–14." For war against Napoleon. Brass   Size 18

25 215 AUSTRIA. Maltese Cross. Arms frosted. A double-headed eagle embossed on centre. Br. gilt. Very fine   Size 22

16 216 AUSTRIA. Head of Francis Joseph; rev. "2 December, 1873." Br. gilt.   Size 23

15 217 AUSTRIA. Duplicate

16 218 ANHALT. Crowned arms over wreath; rev. "1848, Alex. Carl, 1849," in 3 lines, ins. surrounding. Brass proof with ring   Size 19

75 219 AUSTRIA. Maltese Cross, encircled by wreath enameled in green. V. T. on a boss in centre. Silvered, with loop   Size 22

15 220 AUSTRIA. Similar. A large V on boss. Silvered, with loop   Size 22

12 221 BAVARIA. Maltese Cross. Crowned lion on boss; rev. for years 1813–14, with ring and ribbon. Struck from captured cannon. For officers   Size 11

20 222 BAVARIA. Iron Cross. Lion on boss; rev. 1849 in brass letters. Iron, brass rim   Size 24

12 223 Similar Cross for 1866   Same size

10 224 Same for Officers   Size 9

180 225 ENGLAND. Bust of the Prince Regent; rev. Victory seated; Wellington above, Waterloo, June 18, 1815, below. Silver. Scratched   Size 23

210 226 ENGLAND. Head to l.; "Victoria Vindex"; rev. "CABUL 1842," with bar and ribbon. Silver. Very good.   Size 23

300 227 ENGLAND. CRIMEA Medal. Head of Victoria to r.; rev. Victory crowning a Warrior. "Crimea" in field, with four clasps, inscribed SEBASTOPOL, INKERMANN, BALAKLAVA and ALMA. Name on edge. Silver. Fine; rare Size 23

40 228 ENGLAND. Same. Officer's size. Silver   Size 12

2 / 0 229 ENGLAND. Head of Victoria to r.; rev. Victory crowning a naked Warrior, with one bar inscribed NORTHWEST FRONTIER. Name on edge. Silver. Very fine Size 23

2 4/5 230 ENGLAND. Rev. same. Bar inscribed PEGU. Silver. Name on edge. Fine Size 23

2 / 5 231 ENGLAND. Head; rev. Britannia and Lion. "India 1857–58." DELHI on bar. Name on edge. Silver. Very fine Size 23

3 5 232 ENGLAND. Rev. trophy "CHINA." With two bars. PEKIN, 1860. TAKU FORTS, 1860. Name on edge. Silver. Fine Size 23

5 0 233 ENGLAND. 1854. BALTIC medal. Officer's size. No ribbon. Very fine. Silver Size 11

2 0 234 ENGLAND. 1882. EGYPT. Officer's size. TEL-EL-KEBER on bar. Silver. Very fine Size 8 .

3 5 235 FRANCE. ST. HELENA MEDAL. Crowned wreath. Head of Napoleon; rev. inscription. Bronze, oval. Fine. Size 30x32

3 5 236 FRANCE. Same. Very fine

/ 8 237 FRANCE. Same; for Officers. Br. gilt Size 12x20

3 3 0 238 FRANCE. Order of the Lily. Louis XVIII. 1814. Five pointed star in white enamel, gold centre, knobbed points. Head to r.; rev. silver lily on gold field, blue border, suspended from a silver crown by a silver lily. Silver, gold and enamel. Rare Size 12x20

' 3 0 239 FRANCE. Head to l. in cavo-relievo. Louis "Napoleon" in gold, on blue enameled ring ; rev. "Valeur et discipline," surrounded by a heavy wreath. Solid eagle above. Silver gilt Size 17x27

/ 3 5 240 FRANCE. Head to l.; rev. "EXPEDITION DE CHINE, 1860." Names of battles, Ta Kou; Chang-Kia-Wan, etc. Chinese characters on ribbon. Silver proof. Rare Size 20

5 0 241 FRANCE. Same. Officer's size. Silver proof Size 11

/ 5 5 242 FRANCE. Rev. "EXPEDITION DU MEXIQUE 1862-1865." Names of battles, Cumbres, Cerro Borrego, San Lorenzo, etc. Mexican eagle on ribbon. Silver proof. Rare Size 20

6 5 243 FRANCE. Same. Officer's medal. Silver proof. Rare Size 10

4 8 0 244 FRANCE. LEGION OF HONOR. Star of 5 arms and 10 points enameled in white. Gold medallion in centre with blue enamel border. Head of Napoleon I. " Bonaparte, Premier Consul "; rev. Eagle. "Honneur et Patrie." Cross surrounded by wreath, enameled in green, suspended from a silver gilt crown. Fine and rare. For officers and commanders Size 28x44

1 0 0 245 FRANCE. Same, for Knights. Cross and wreath not gilded. Several checks in enamel. Fine; rare Size 20x34

5 0 246 FRANCE. LEGION OF HONOR. Charles X. 1825. Similar star. Head of Henry IV.; rev. 3 fleur de lis "Honneur et Patrie" surrounding; suspended from a silver crown. Fine Size 20x31

4 5 247 FRANCE. LEGION OF HONOR. Louis Philippe. Similar star. Head of Henry IV. on gold boss. Blue enamel border; rev. two flags; "Honneur et Patrie" in gold letters on blue enamel; suspended from a crown. Silver. Fine Size 13x23

4 7 5 248 FRANCE. LEGION OF HONOR. Napoleon I., 1802. Similar star. Head to r. "Napoleon Emp. des Française."; rev. Eagle, suspended from a silver crown. Silver, gold and enamel. Some nicks in the enamel. Fine; rare. Size 14x25

2 2 5 249 FRANCE. LEGION OF HONOR. Republic of 1848. Head of Napoleon. "Bonaparte premier Consul, 19 Mai, 1802 "; rev. 2 flags crossed, red, white and blue enamel, gold ground. "Honneur et Patrie" in raised letters. "Republic Francaise " in gold letters on blue enamel, surrounding with ring. No crown. Fine and rare. Size 24

5 5 250 FRANCE. Ambulance Corps Cross, 1870, 71. Square cross, cross on ribbon. Bronze. Fine; rare. Size 24

3 5 251 FRANCE. Same. Reduced. Size 12

1 2 252 FRANCE. Same. No cross on ribbon. Minute. Size 8

2 5 253 HANOVER. Medal for Battle of Langensalza. Head of Geo. V. to left; rev. "Langensalza, 27 Juni, 1866 " in wreath. Name on edge. Brass. Size 23

1 3 0 254 HANSEATIC LEAGUE, 1813–1814. The Arms of Hamburg, Bremen and Lubeck leaning against the stump of an oak. " God with us " above; rev. " Hanseatic Legion," etc. Silver. Very fine. Size 23

/2 255 HESSE. Medal for Wars against France, 1814–15 ; rev. "K. W. II. to his brave Hessians, 1821." Very good. Size 19

/5 256 HOLLAND. Army Medal for 12 years' service. Shield of arms and trophy "Voor Truwen Dienst ; " rev. large w on a crowned ermine. Bronze. Fine. Size 23

/8 257 ITALY. Papal Medal. Arms ; rev. ins. 1849. Br. No ring or ribbon. Fine. Size 20

2.2 258 ITALY. Papal Cross, 1867. Arms. "Fidei et Virtuti." Long cross. "Hine Victoria." Composition metal. Fine. Size 26x31

/8 259 OLDENBURG. Medal of 1866. Head of the Grand Duke Nicholas to l.; rev. 1866 in wreath. Bronze gilt. Proof. Size 19

/3 260 OLDENBURG. Same, for officers. Br., gilt. Proof. Size 10

/0 261 PRUSSIA. Medal for duty. Cross. Eagle in centre. "Von Fels Zum Meer ; " rev. "Frederick Wilhelm IV., 1848– 1849 ' in four lines. "To his warriors faithful unto death" surrounding, copper gilt.—And one bust ; rev. monogram. 17 Marz, 1865. Brass. Size 20 2 pcs

// 262 PRUSSIA. Same for officers. Copper gilt. Proof. Size 10

/0 263 PRUSSIA. Medal for Military Valor. Monogram under two crowns ; rev. 1864, and rev. "Unsern Tapfern Kriegern, 1864," in wreaths. Copper gilt and steel proofs. Size 19 2 pcs

/40 264 PRUSSIA. DUPPEL CROSS. Danish Campaign. Cross encircled by a wreath. Head of King William ; rev. Eagle on cannon. Duppel, 18 Apr., 1864, in angles of cross. Silver proof. Size 21

/7 265 PRUSSIA. Same, for officers. Silver proof. Size 9

/5 266 PRUSSIA. ALSEN CROSS. Similar cross; rev. Prussian Eagle with wreath over a vessel. "Alsen, 29 Jun. 1864 " in arms. Copper gilt. Very fine. Size 21

// 267 PRUSSIA. Austrian campaign. Similar cross, monogram. etc.; rev. Eagle on cannon. Koniggratz Den, 3 Juli 1866 ; rev. Treuen Kriegern, 1866. Copper gilt proof. Sizes 23(2) and 12 3 pcs

55 268 PRUSSIA. IRON CROSS, 1879. Inner cross iron, Arms and back silvered. W under Crown, 1870, below. Without loop. Very fine, largest size. Size 37

/2,5 269 PRUSSIA. Iron Cross. Silver edges. F. W. under crown, a sprig of oak in centre. 1813 below; rev. W under a crown. 1870 below. Very fine. Size 27

/2 270 PRUSSIA. Maltese Cross, inscribed 1870–1771; rev. W crowned, "For fidelity to duty." Steel proof. Size 19

/3 271 RUSSIA. Medal for Crimean War, 1853–4–5–6; rev. inscription in Russian. Yellow and dark bronze. Very good. Size 18　　　　　　　　　　　　　　　　　2 pcs

/00 272 RUSSIA. CROSS OF ST. GEORGE. Monogram on shield in centre; rev. St. George and the Dragon. Silver. Fine and rare. Size 23

/00 273 ROUMANIA. IRON CROSS. 1877. For the defense of the Danube, C. C. I. in monogram crowned; rev. "Tregerea Dunarii, 1877." Borders burnished. Fine; rare. Size 28

/5 274 SAXONY. Maltese Cross, frosted centre, burnished border, monogram crowned; rev. 1866 in wreath. Copper gilt. Size 18

/2 275 Saxony. Medal for long and faithful service, A. F. A. in monogram crowned within wreath; rev. inscription in wreath. Copper gilt. Proof. Size 19

FOREIGN SILVER AND COPPER.

/15 276 Frankfurt. Double Thaler, 1866, commonly called the Janauschek Thaler. Uncirculated

85 277 Mexico. Maximilian Dollar, 1867. Fair

20 278 Mexico. Maximilian Half Dollar, Dime and Half Dime, 1866. Good　　　　　　　　　　　　　　　　3 pcs

47 279 Hawaii. King Kalakaua I., 1883, head to r.; rev. Arms. Akahi Dala, Hapalua, Hapaha and Umi Keneta, or dollar, half, quarter and dime. Fine　　　　　　　　　4 pcs

/2 280 James II. Gun Money. XXX. May, 1690; Aug. and Oct. 1689; XII. Jan., Aug., Sep., and Oct, 1689 and May, 1690. Good lot　　　　　　　　　　　　　　　　8 pcs

7/5 281 Foreign Coppers, half-penny and farthing size. Ordinary 25 pcs

..AMERICAN SILVER DOLLARS.

/30 282 1795. Flowing hair. H. No. 5. Rare variety. Good

/60 283 1795. Flowing hair. H. No. 7. Rare variety. Fine

4 1796. Large date, a slight break in rev. die between I and
C of America. Very fine
5 1798. 13 stars, small eagle, a scratch across the head on obv.
Good; rare
6 1799. H. No. 16. Fine
7 1799. 5 stars facing. H. No. 23. Good; scarce
8 1802. H. No. 5. A deep nick on neck, otherwise fine.
9 1836. Flying Eagle. Very good; a slight bruise on edge.
Scarce
0 1836. Flying Eagle. Fine; a small plug neatly inserted
above the head
1 1842. Fine
2 1848. Fine
3 1855. Slightly scratched proof. Scarce
4 1873. Brilliant proof
5 1881. Trade. Brilliant proof
6 1883. Standard. O. Mint. Uncirculated, and brilliant
mint lustre. Scarce

HALF DOLLARS.

7 1794. Cracked die, 21 berries in wreath. Fair for date.
Scarce
8 1795. H. No. 1. Good
9 1795. H. No. 2. Good
0 1795. H. No. 3. Very fair
1 1795. H. No. 5. Good
2 1795. H. No. 7. Very fair
3 1795. H. No. 8. Good
4 1795. H. No. 9. Good
5 1795. H. No. 10. Very fair
6 1795. H. No. 11. Very fair
7 1795. H. No. 16. Poor, scratched and much worn
8 1795. H. No. 18. Poor. Very rare
9 1795. H. No. 24. Very fair
0 1795. H. No. 26. Nearly good
1 1801. Good
2 1802. Good
3 1803. Very good
4 1811. Uncirculated

1 80 315 1815. Fair for date.   Scarce
2 60 316 1815. Very good
  60 317 1817. Over 1813.   Good
  50 318 1827. Uncirculated
  50 319 1830. Uncirculated
  90 320 1834. Large date. Small letters. Uncirculated
  50 321 1836. Head of 1835. Lettered edge. Fine
2 60 322 1836. Milled edge. Very fine. Scarce
  60 323 1839. Fine
  80 324 1851. Very good. O Mint. Scarce
  60 325 1851. Fair. O Mint
1 75 326 1852. Very good. Scaree
  50 327 1866. Without motto. S. Mint. Very fair
  55 328 1878. Slightly tarnished proof
  50 329 1879. Uncirculated. Proof surface
  55 330 1880. Uncirculated. Proof surface

QUARTER DOLLARS.

2 00 331 1796. Very fair for date.   Scarce
2 5 332 1806. Good
2 5 333 1815. Very fair
2 5 334 1838. Good
2 5 335 1847. Very good
2 5 336 1853. Good
4 2 5 337 1853. Without arrows. Good; scarce
  30 338 1861. Proof *tarnished*
  30 339 1862. Uncirculated
  35 340 1872. Brilliant proof
  36 341 1873. Uncirculated
  47 342 1874. With arrows. Brilliant proof
  46 343 1879. Brilliant proof
  27 344 1880. Uncirculated

DIMES.

1 60 345 1796. Broken die. Very good. Scarce
2 1 346 1796. Perfect die. Poor
1 35 347 1798. Very fair for date

1798, 1801, 3, 5. Barely fair and fair.   One pierced (1801)
4 pcs
1805, 7 and 11.   Very fair   3 pcs
1807, 9, 11.   Barely fair   3 pcs
1814.   Large date.   Very good
1814.   A small date.   Good
1824, fair ; '35, good ; '38 without stars, O Mint, and '53
without arrows.   Ordinary   4 pcs
1846.   Very good
1846.   Fair for date
1860.   S Mint with stars.   Scarce
1860, 73, 79, 80.   Uncirculated   4 pcs
1871.   Brilliant proof

HALF DIMES AND PROOF SETS.

1794.   Very fair for date.   H. No. 1.   Scarce
1794.   Very good for date.   H. No. 3.   Pierced
1795.   Good.   H. No. 1.   Perfect die
1795.   Very fair.   H. No. 1.   Broken die
1795.   Very good.   H. No. 2
1795.   Good, slightly bent and bruised.   H. No. 3.   Rare
variety
1795.   Very fair.   H. No. 4.   Rare variety
1796.   Fair
1797.   15 stars.   Good
1797.   16 stars.   Good
1800.   Good
1800.   LIBERTY.   Very good.   Pin scratched
1801.   Good.   A few scratches on obv
1803.   Large date.   H. No. 1.   Very fair
1803.   Small date.   H. No. 2.   Poor.   Pierced
1838.   Without stars.   O Mint.   Very good for date
1844.   Very fine.   Scarce
1845, 53, 7, 8, 60, 61.   Fine and uncirculated   6 pcs
1846.   Fair.   Pierced
1867, 73.   Brilliant proofs   2 pcs
1851, 5, 9, 60, 1, 2 and 1851.   O Mint.   Three-Cent pieces.
Good   7 pcs

	380	Base Money set.	1866.	Uncirculated.	5, 3, 2, 1	4 pcs
52						
40	381	Base Money set.	1867.	Uncirculated.	5, 3, 2, 1	4 pcs
36	382	Base Money set.	1868.	Uncirculated.	5, 3, 2, 1	4 pcs
35	383	Base Money set.	1869.	Uncirculated.	5, 3, 2, 1	4 pcs
30	384	Base Money set.	1870.	Uncirculated.	5, 3, 2, 1	4 pcs
31	385	Base Money set.	1871.	Uncirculated.	5, 3, 2, 1	4 pcs

CENTS.

2 50 386 1793. Flowing hair. Wreath. Planchet cracked at edge, otherwise pretty good

2 15 387 1793. Flowing hair. Chain. Barely fair

1 95 388 1793. Flowing hair. Chain. Barely fair. Corroded

36 389 1794. M. No. 9. Very fair. Light olive brown

36 390 1794. M. No. 16. Good. Dark color. Slightly corroded

110 391 1794. M. No. 17. Fine. Even dark color

70 392 1794. M. No. 21. Good. Obv. red; rev. brown. Has been burnished

16 393 1794. M. No. 32. Barely fair

20 394 1794. M. No. 32. A variety. Fair

95 395 1794. M. No. 32. Perfect die. Good. Dark

16 396 1794. M. No. 36. Barely fair

20 397 1794. Varieties. Fair and barely fair

45 398 1795. Thin die. Good

65 399 1796. Liberty Cap. Good for date. Small piece clipped from edge of planchet

55 400 1797. Dark brown color. Very good

40 401 1798. Even brown color. Good

105 402 1801. Rich brown color. Very good

55 403 1802. Dark steel color. Good

60 404 1803. Dark brown color. Very good

310 405 1804. Fair. Bent and Scratched. The 0 in date damaged

27 406 1806-8 (2). Fair   3 pcs

225 407 1809. Very good for date. Scarce

75 408 1809. ~~Fair~~ for date *poor*

30 409 1810. Brown color. Good

50 410 1811. Perfect die. Fair

55 411 1811. 11 over 10. Very fair

18 412 1813. Fair   2 pcs

60 413 1814. Crossed 4. Very fine. Dark even color
2 2 0 414 1814. Standless 4. *Double chin.* Rich dark brown color. Uncirculated. Rare in this condition
/2 415 1814. Both varieties. Very fair   2 pcs
// 416 1815. Altered from 1845. Good
JJ 417 1816. Broken die. Rich olive brown. Uncirculated
J¯0 418 1817. 13 stars. Uncirculated. Red
20 419 1817. 15 stars. Fair
JO 420 1818. Rich steel color. Perfect die. Very fine
26 421 1819. Golden bronze color. Very fine *cleaned*
46 422 1820. Connected Stars. Uncirculated. Golden
/J¯ 423 1820. Perfect die. Dark color. Good
/6 424 1821–5. Fair and good   2 pcs
J¯ 425 1822. Good
26 426 1823. Perfect date. Dark color. Corroded
7 0 427* 1826. Rich iridescent color. Fine *cleaned*
60 428 1827. Rich brown color. Almost uncirculated
90 429 1828. Fine brown color. Very fine
/0 430 1832. Dark brown, nearly black color. Slight corrosion. Fine
J¯0 431 1834. Connected stars. Rich brown color. Scarcely any marks of circulation. Very fine
30 432 1836. Golden brown color. All the ᴇ's in legend of rev. broken. Fine
40 433 1837 Connected stars. Rich brown color. Fine
60 434 1838 Uncirculated. Red
4J¯ 435 1839 over 1836. Fair. Rare
7 436 1839 Head of 1840. Olive brown. Very good
4J¯ 437 1840 Purple color. Very good
/0 438 1842 Brown. Good
/J¯ 439 1843 Type of 1842. Very good
/8 440 1844 Steel color. Very good
JJ¯ 441 1845 Barely circulated, traces of red remaining
8J¯ 442 1846 Rich brown color. Fine
JJ¯ 443 1847 Fine brown color. Very good
40 444 1848 Uncirculated. Red
JJ¯ 445 1849 Fine brown color. Nearly uncirculated
3J¯ 446 1850 Uncirculated. Red
3J¯ 447 1851 Olive brown color. Fine

2 6 448 1852 Uncirculated. Brown. Red showing
3 1 449 1853 Uncirculated. Golden *cleaned*
2 5 450 1856 Rich purple color. Uncirculated
40 451 1857 Large date. Uncirculated. Red
35 452 1857 Small date. Uncirculated. Brown and red *partly*
1 ½ 453 Bronze Cents. 1864 (6), '73 (4), '74 (3), '79 (3), '80 (2), '8
     (4), '82, '83, '84. Uncirculated   25 p
5 0 454 Nickel Cents. 1858. Large flying eagle; rev. oak wreat
     with and without shield, and tobacco wreath. . India
     head. 4 reverses. Proofs   7 p
5 455 Two Cents. 1864 (4), '65 (5), '68. Uncirculated   10 p

HALF CENTS.

1 6 0 456 1793 Dark color. Everything plain. Slight corrosio
     Fine for date. F. No. 1
2 3 0 457 1793 Good brown color. Everything plain. Very goo
     F. No. 2
1 1 5 458 1793 Light brown color. Very fair. F. No. 3 *scratche*
2 1 459 1794 Very good. W stamped on head. F. No. 1
3 2 460 1794 Good. Dark color. F. No. 4
5 0 461 1794 Nearly black. Very good. F. No. 5 *corroded*
1 1 5 462 1795 Thick planchet. Very good
40 463 1795 Thin planchet. Brown color. Good for date *nick*
10.25 464 1796 Broken die. Everything plain except the HALF
     rev. A very desirable specimen of this rare date. Gua
     anteed
35 465 1797 Very good. F. No. 1 *scratched*
2 2 466 1797 Fair. A variety not in Frossard's list. Very bro
     milling
4 467 1800, 3, 5, 8. Fair   4 p
1 2 5 468 1802 Very fair. Scarce
9 0 469 1802 Fair for date.
7 470 1804 Plain 4. No stems to wreath. Straight $\frac{1}{200}$. Ve
     good
3 0 471 1804 Crossed 4, with protruding tongue and chin. Curv
     $\frac{1}{200}$. Very fair
1 0 472 1806 With and without stems to wreath. Good.   2 p

16 473 1807 Good color. ALF. in half on rev., united at bottom. Good. Scarce variety

*474 1809 Nearly black. Good

25 475 1810 Fine brown color. Very good

33 476 1810 Dark color. Good

32 477 1811 Very fair

35 478 1825 Rich brown color. ~~Uncirculated.~~ Proof surface

22 479 1826 Fine light brown color. ~~Uncirculated.~~ Proof surface

31 480 1828 13 stars. Beautiful purple color. Uncirculated and brilliant

15 481 1829 Fine iridescent color. Very fine

17 482 1832 Olive brown color. ~~Uncirculated~~

4 483 1833, 4, 5, 28. 12 stars. Very good   4 pcs

25 484 1837 Half-cent's worth of pure copper. Good

10 485 1840 Uncirculated. Very fine. Electrotype

620 486 1847 Proof. Mint restrike. Rare

37 487 1849 Rich olive brown color. ~~Uncirculated.~~ Rare in this condition *spotted*

13 488 1850, 1, 3, 4, 5 and 6. Uncirculated   6 pcs

620 489 1852. Steel color. Proof. Rare

10 490 1857. Uncirculated

COLONIALS—CONNECTICUT CENTS.

Arranged according to Crosby's list.

80 491 1787. Horned bust. Olive brown. Very fine. 4 L.

15 492 1787. Horned bust. Dark color. Very fair. A variety. 4 L.

10 493 1787. Fair. Rare. 6 M.

12 494 1787. Very good, but slightly corroded. 31 R.

12 495 1787. Very good. *Green patination* on obv. 33 Z.

5 496 1787. Good, pierced. 33 R.

11 497 1787. Very fair. 37 K.

11 498 1788. Head to r. Good. Corroded. 2 D*.

NEW JERSEY CENTS.

Arranged according to Dr. Maris' list.

52 499 1786. Very fine. Olive brown color. 14 J.
15 500 1786. Very good. Covered with green patina. 16 L.
25 501 1786. Very good. 18 M.
35 502 1786. Good. 20 N. Rare variety
18 503 1786. Good. 21 N.
9 504 1786. Barely-fair, 14 J. (2), and good, 23 R.   3 pcs
15 505 1787. Very fair. 39 A.
11 506 1787. Fair. 38 C.
5 507 1787. Poor. 6 D.
9 508 1787. Fair. 43 D. and 46 E., 2 varieties, and 48 G., 2 varieties. Fair   5 pcs
15 509 1787. Very good. Golden. 48 G. *cleaned*
9 510 1787. 54 K., 24 P. and 63 S. Very fair and good.   3 pcs
25 511 1787. Very good. Dark color. 62 Q.
9 512 1787. 32 T., 64 T., 56 U. Very fair   3 pcs
15 513 1787. Brown color. Very good. Small planchet. 64 T. Rare variety
11 514 1787. Very fair, 38 V.; 1788, barely fair, 67 V.   2 pcs
15 515 1723 Wood's Half-Penny; and Fugio "States United." Very fair   2 pcs
170 516 1791 Washington Cent. Large eagle. Very good
43/4 517 Colonials—Conn., N. J., Wood's Half-Penny, Fugio, etc. Mostly poor. 3 pierced   31 pcs
3 518 Hard Times Tokens, arranged according to Haseltine's list. Nos. 1, 2, 6, 10, 11, 15, 17, 18, 19, 20, 1, 5, 6, 7, 9 (2), 31, 4, 5, 6, 8, 9 (2), 40, 4, 5, 6, 7, 9, 50, 1, 3, 4, 60, 6, 8, 9, 84, 5, 7, 8, 9, 92, 4, 100, 1, 2 and 111. All in envelopes, properly numbered. Condition generally good. 2 pierced. 48 pcs
1/4 519 Rebellion Token or Copperheads, a variety; and four Medallets in brass and w. m. Good. 4 pierced - 37 pcs.

COIN BOOKS AND COIN CATALOGUES.

30 520 Pinkerton, John. Essay on Medals. 4 plates of Ancient Coins. 2 vols, 12mo, calf, gilt extra. Lond. 1789

Snowden, J. Ross. Description of the Medals of Washington, of National and Miscellaneous Medals, &c., in the Museum of the Mint. To which are added Biographical Notices of the Directors of the Mint from 1792 to 1851. Illustrated by 79 fac-simile engravings, 4to, cloth, gilt. Phila. 1861

Dickeson, M. W. American Numismatic Manual. With 29 plates. 2d edition. 4to, cloth (binding injured). Phila. 1860

Bushnell, C. I. Catalogue of the Collection of. Priced in ink

Fewsmith Catalogue, Oct. 4, 1870. Priced

American Journal of Numismatics. Vol. 1. Complete. 12 Nos.

Lot of Foreign Catalogues of Coins. 2 priced   19 pcs

Lot of Miscellaneous Numismatic and Autographic Literature   50 pcs

Maris, Dr. Edwar. Varieties of the Copper Issues of the United States Mint in the Year 1794. Corrected in ink to correspond with the 2d edition. 12mo, paper. Phila. 1869

W. Elliot Woodward's Sixth Semi-Annual Sale, New York, March 20 to 25, 1865. Priced. Rare

Lot of Priced Catalogues of Various Sales, from 1870 to 1883   41

ENGLISH AND AMERICAN COPPER.

1797 George II. Two-penee. Legend incused. Nearly fine

Half-penny. Token of T. Hall, Taxidermist, ins.; rev. a peculiar bird, like a Pelican, on a tree. Proof surface. Very fine

Belleville Token. J. Gibbs. A very good specimen of this rare card

Liberia Cent, 1833. Very good

Spain. Head of Isabella; rev. arms. 8 M. Rich dark brown color. Uncirculated. Half-penny size

Liberia, 1847. Two cents. Good

11 538 A complete set of the Baron Goertz Dalers. All in very
good condition. Scarce as a set   10 pcs
16 539 Ceylon. Two Stivers, 1815.—And Lady Godiva half-penny,
1794. Ordinary   2 pcs
9 540 Magdalen Island, Walsall, Hilston and four other penny
tokens. Very good and uncirculated   7 pcs
6 541 J. Lackington. Half-penny, 1794. Uncirculated. Golden
2 542 Ships, Colonies and Commerce; Guernesey 4 Doubles, and
Newfoundland Cent. Good   3 pcs
5 543 Am I not a Woman and a Sister? Politicals of Verplanck
and Scott; and two Hard Times Tokens. Good.   5 pcs
30 544 Nero; rev. the temple of Janus closed. Fine green patination. Very good. M. B.
31 545 Maxentius. Patinated. M. B.
8 546 Vespasian. Various types. Barely fair. One pierced.
6 pcs
7 547 Caracalla (2 varieties), Sept. Severus (2) and Trajan Decius.
Fair   5 pcs
75 548 Brutus. Head; rev. cap and daggers. Very good. Not
genuine
6 549 Nero. Greek Imp. Tetradrachm, billon, and two Greek
copper coins. Poor; rare   3 pcs
7/8 550 War Tokens, or Copperheads. A great variety. Good condition   250 pcs
1½ 551 Beer checks, toll checks, hotel check, etc. Brass. About
5-cent size. Good lot   34 pcs
3½ 552 Store cards. Gilt backs. Containing mirrors. Two of
them perforated on the side for pins. Size 24   7 pcs
1¼ 553 Store cards. Brass shells. Various. Two containing tin
types. Fine lot. Size 22   15 pcs
30 554 1794 Cent. Very fair
30 555 1794 Cent. Very good, but covered with a deep corrosion
35 556 1794 Cent. Good
35 557 1794 Cent. Good. Dark Color
50 558 1794 Cent. Good
The above five '94 cents are varieties.
5 559 1817 Cent. Even dark color. Good
10 560 1828 Large date. Olive brown color. Nearly uncirculated
50 561 1793 Nova Constellatio. V. S. type. Brown. Fine

45 562 Rosa Americana Penny, 1723. Crowned rose. Fair
19 563 New Jersey Cent, 1787. Very good. Dark color
95 564 Washington Cent, 1791. Large eagle. Very fair
41 565 Connecticut Cent, 1787. Horned bust. Very good
18 566 Connecticut Cent, 1787. Head of George III. Fair.
Scarce
17 567 Connecticut Cent. Negro head. Good
15 568 Connecticut Cent, 1787. Young head. Very fair
15 569 Connecticut Cent. Head to r. Good
25 570 Connecticut Cent, 1788. Even black color. Very good.
Scarce variety
16 571 Vermont Cent. Head to r. Very fair
60 572 Medal. Bust of James Ross Snowden. ¾ face to l.;
rev. view of the Philadelphia mint. In very high relief.
Solid Electrotype. Very fine. Size 51
35 573 Quinnipiach Medal. View of the Puritans praying at Quinnipiach, 1638. "The Desert shall rejoice;" rev. view of
New Haven, 1838. "And blossom as the rose." Very
fine; rare Size 36
11 574 Henry G. Sampson's Card. W. m. proof Size 27
18 575 Centennial Award Medal. Phila., 1876. W. m. proof
Size 34

SILVER.

85 576 Ragusa. Episcopal Dollar. 1767. Bust of the Bishop;
rev. Arms. Good
110 577 Saxony. Double Thaler of John V. 1859. Fine
700 578 Giovanni B. Vico. Fine bust to r.; rev. Science seated
holding a torch, View of Naples and Mt. Etna in the distance; in ex. VII. Congresso degli Scienziati Italiani 1845.
Proof. Several scratches on obv. A beautiful medal.
Weighs 5 ozs. Silver Size 38
60 579 Medal. Obv. Coat-of-Arms, a bird with a fish in its beak
on a shield, crown above, two lions for supporters;
rev. Fortune and Justice with rudder and scale, "Con-
cordia" above, in ex. S. C. Fine Size 24
35 580 Sweden. Chas. XIV. Bust; rev. Tomb; Oscar I. Head;
rev. View of Church (?). Good 2 pcs

35 581 Sweden.   Chas. XIV.   Head ; rev. Agricultural Scene.
Very good   Size 20

40 582 Mexico.   Maximilian Half-Dollar.   1866.   Good

27 583 Austria. 1 Florin of Francis Joseph, and 500 and 1,000 Reis
of Brazil.   Good   3 pcs

25 584 England.   Geo. III.   Sixpence. 1787.   Proof

18 585 England.   Geo. III.   Same.   Sixpence of George IV. 1821;
rare rev. and 10 Cents Hong Kong of Victoria.   Good
3 pcs

45 586 England.   War Medal.   Crimea.   With loop.   Officer's
Medal   Size 11

4.10 587 1652.   Oak-Tree Shilling ; split trunk.   Obv. good ; rev.
fine.   Scarce

180 588 1795.   Dollar.   Somewhat rubbed, but a fine, heavy, sharp
dollar, with an almost proof lustre.   A very desirable
piece

100 589 1853.   Dollar.   Good

105 590 1878.   Dollar.   Standard; the first die; 8 feathers in the
eagle's tail.   Proof

60 591 1795.   Half-Dollar.   Very fair ; might be called " good,
for date "

50 592 1803.   Half-Dollar.   Good

250 593 1796.   Quarter-Dollar.   Good; rare

35 594 1804.   Quarter-Dollar.   Poor ; pierced

80 595 1818.   Quarter-Dollar.   Uncirculated and sharp.   Slight
tarnish on obv

25 596 1818.   Quarter-Dollar.   Very good

25 597 1879.   Quarter-Dollar.   Uncirculated ; brilliant

25 598 1879.   Quarter-Dollar.   Uncirculated ; brilliant

42 599 1801.   Dime.   Poor

10 600 1814.   Dime.   Very fair

10 601 1879 (3), '81, '82 (2), and 83, Dimes.   Uncirculated.
7 pcs

75 602 Pattern Nickel Set, 1868.   5, 3 and 1 Cent Nickel.   Proof
Rare   3 pcs

5 603 1883.   Five Cents Nickel, with " Cents " on rev.   Proof
3 pcs

525 604 Dickeson's American Numismatic Manual, illustrated by 19
plates of fac-similes of coins and Indian antiquities.   The
coins in proper color.   4to, cloth.   Philadelphia, 1859

COINS OF CANADA.

Arranged according to Sandham's list.   All are half-pennies unless otherwise mentioned.

2, 605 Bust of the Duke of Wellington.   Half-penny token, 1816; rev. ship under sail to r.   Montreal.   Good.   S. 12

3 606 Ship under sail to r.   " Half-penny token, Upper Canada;" rev. an anvil, two spades crossed above.   Very fair.   S. 14 and S. 15.   Varieties   2 pcs

8 607 Obv. Canada.   1830; rev. Half-penny, in two lines.   S. 21. —And obv. same as lot 606; rev. a plough, " To facilitate trade " (2).   S. 23.   Good   3 pcs

42, 608 " Francis Mullin & Sons," &c.; rev. ship in full sail to r. "Commerce token."   Very good.   S. 32

5 609 Anvil with hammer and tongs between scythe and vise, two crossed spades above; rev. T. S. Brown & Co., Importers, &c.   Very fair.   S. 35.   Obv. bouquet; rev. Un Sou. S. 40.   Good   2 pcs

3 610 Boquet; rev. Un Sou.   Good.   S. 44, 45, 47 and 48. Good   4 pcs

3 611 Similar.   S. No. 54, 60, 62, 64.   Good   4 pcs

3 612 Similar.   S. No. 68, 71, 74.   Very fair   3 pcs

10 613 Rebellion Token.   S. No. 75.   Good.   Scarce

17 614 Belleville Token.   " T. Duseman, Butcher."   Good

6 615 Canada, 1841; rev. " Half-penny " in two lines."   Good

3 616 Canada Bank Token, 1854.   St. George and the dragon; rev. Arms.   Penny Token, size 88, and half-penny tokens, S. 89   7 pcs

3 617 Figure.   Province du Canada.   Deux Sous; rev. arms of Quebec, 1852, one penny.   S. 90.   Half-Penny, same. S. 91.   Head of Victoria; rev. One Cent.   Various dates. S. 92 and 93.   Good lot   5 pcs

55 618 Head of Victoria.   " Dominion of Canada, Province of Quebec "; rev. in beaded circle, " Use Devins Vegetable Worm Pastilles, July 1st, 1867."   Outside of Circle, "Devins & Bolton, Druggists, Montreal."   Very good. ~~Very rare~~.   S. 95

Mr. Sandham says that the coins were made in Birmingham, and on their arrival in Canada they were seized by the authorities; the *New Currency Act* forbidding the manufacture or importation of coins or tokens.   It will thus be seen that the coin is of great rarity.

/ 30 619 Montreal and Lachine Railroad. Locomotive; rev. beaver, "Third class." Round hole in centre. Good. S. 3.
"Miscellaneous"

/ 620 Fisheries and agriculture; rev. One Cent, 1855. S. Mis. 17 (2), and three others unplaced   5 pcs

1/2 621 Hibernia seated. One Half-Penny Token, 1820; rev. ship. Trade and Navigation. S. "doubtful" 8 (2). Eagle "Half-Penny Token"; rev. seated figure within wreath. S. "doubtful" 15, others 18 (2), 21, 25 (4), and North American Token. S. "doubtful" 27. Very fair.   11 pcs

/ 7 622 Vessel under sail to r. "Ships, Colonies and Commerce;" rev. "For Publick Accommodation," in 3 lines. Very fair for the piece. ~~Excessively rare~~. S. "doubtful" 30

6 623 Vessel ; rev. "Wellington, Waterloo, 1815," in 3 lines. Scarce. S. doubtful, 35

3 624 Bust in Uniform. "Victoria Nobis est;" rev. figure, "Half-Penny Token." S. "doubtful" 47, and two other "doubtful" 51 and 52. Penny tokens. Good.   3 pcs

3/4 625 "Ships, Colonies and Commerce;" rev. ship. Good. 13 pcs

2-6 626 MAGDALEN ISLAND. Seal; rev. codfish. S. 1

5 627 NEWFOUNDLAND. Arms; rev. a fleece suspended. "R. and I. S. Rutherford," &c. S. No. 6 (2) 7, 8. Good 4 pcs

/ 3 627* New Foundland. Rutherford's Card No. 9. Large letters. Scarce

/ 628 NEW BRUNSWICK, 1843. Head of Victoria; rev. ship. Penny and half-penny, two of each, good, the half-pennies fine. S. 1 and 2   4 pcs

1/2 629 Similar set. Penny and half-pennies, 1854, and half cent, 1861. S. 3, 4 and 6.   5 pcs

/ 630 PRINCE EDWARD'S ISLAND. "Speed the plough;" rev. "success to fisheries." S. 2 (4); rev. "self-government and free trade," 1855 and 7. S. 3 (2), 4 (8), and 5. Very good and fine.   16 pcs

6 631 Steamship "Half-Penny Token"; rev. "Fisheries and agriculture." Good. S. 6

·3 632 Head to l., 1871 ; rev. Two trees, "Prince Edward's Island, One Cent." Uncirculated. Red

633 Communicant's Token. "St. John, Newbrunswick, 1842";
rev. "St. Stephen's Church, Rev. W. T. Wishart."
Lead. Fine ; excessively rare. S. 16

634 Communicant's Token. "St. Andrew's Church, Stratford,
C. W., 1858"; rev. 1 Cor. XI. 23. Lead. Octagon.
Fine; very rare. S. 14x17

> The lead communicant tokens of Canada are very scarce, espe-
> cially those of St. John, as nearly all the church property was
> destroyed by fire in 1877.

NOVA SCOTIA.

635 " W. L. White's Halifax House, Halifax, Cheap Dry
Goods Store"; rev. "Payable at W. L. White's," etc.
One Farthing. Uncirculated, proof surface. Not in
Sandham. Rare

636 Ship " Halifax Steamboat Company "; rev. " Ferry Token "
in two lines. Bronze. Uncirculated. Very rare. Not
in Sandham

637 1815. Bust ; rev. View of the Government house. Card
of Hosterman & Etter. Good. S. 6. One pierced. 2 pcs

638 1814. Bust of George III. Card of Garrett & Alport,
Halifax. Very good. S. 7

639 1814. Bust of Sir Philip Brooke, commander of the Shannon ; rev. Britannia seated, in the distance view of the
action between the Shannon and the Chesapeake. Varie-
ties. Good. S. 8   3 pcs

640 1816. Card of W. A. & S. Black, Halifax. Keg marked
" Spikes, Nails," etc.; rev. A warehouse. Fine. Red.
S. 11 *Cleaned*

641 1816. Same device, but without name. Very fair. Pierced.
S. 12

642 1815. Bust of Geo. III.; rev. Ship "Halifax." Good.
S. 14

643 1840. Head of Victoria to l.; rev. Thistle. One Penny
Token. Good. S. 17

644 1856. Head of Victoria to l.; rev. Sprig. One Penny
Token. Uncirculated. Golden, mint lustre. S. 19

1 10 645 Half-Penny Token. Ship sailing to r., " Nova Scotia and New Brunswick," below ship " Success '"; rev. Female seated. Somewhat bruised and abused. Fair; rare. S. 21

5 646 Card of J. Brown. Ship ; rev. Thistle with four leaves. Fine. Red. S. 22 *cleaned*

1 2 647 Card of Robert Purves, Wallace ; rev. " Encourage country importers." Very fine; scarce. S. 23

1 648 Lot of Penny and Half-Penny Tokens. S. 2 (2), 9 (2), 15, 16 (5), 18 (2), 19, 20 (2). Good lot   15 pcs

GREEK AND ROMAN BRASS.

7 1/2 649 Panormus, Calens, Neapolis, etc. Good. Small   9 pcs

8 650 Macedon, Himera, Egypt, etc. Fair and very good. 11 pcs

2 5 651 Uncia. Head of Pallas ; rev. Wheel, two fishes surrounding. Very good. S. 17x20

5 0 652 Greek Colonials of various Emperors. Very fine.   6 pcs

8 653 Others. Good to fine   10 pcs

2 0 654 Greek Colonial of Alex. Severus. Bust to r.; rev. Julia reclining on a couch L.A. Very good. Broad. Rare

1 3 655 First brass of Vespasian, Hadrian, Ant. Pius, Gordianus III. (2), Philip, and another. Very fair   8 pcs

1 7 656 Galba ; rev. Liberty standing. G. B. Fine. *Paduan*

1 6 657 Augustus. Fine head to l.; rev. Emperor on estrade, " Adlocut." Good. G. B. *Paduan*

1 7 658 Augustus ; rev. Crocodile, Col. Nem. and M. B. of Nero. Very fair and good   2 pcs

8 659 Germanicus, Domitian and Vespasian (2). M. B. Fair
    4 pcs

6 660 Gordianus III., Philip I., Hadrian, etc. Fair and poor. M. B.   9 pcs

3 661 Rome. Various Emperors and a few Greek. 3d brass. Fair lot   32 pcs

11.2 5 662 Rome. Brass Medallion; obv. Prow. Nine figures on the deck; rev. seated female, a figure on either side; three circles and outer wreath surrounding. Green patination. Very rare. Weight about 9 oz. S. 48

GREEK SILVER.

ALEXANDER. Magnus. Head to left; rev. title and seated Jupiter. Good. Drachm

NEAPOLIS. Macedonia; obv. a grinning mask; rev. a female head. Very fine. Concave. Scarce. Hemi-drachm

ARADUS. Head to right; rev. a galley. Good. Scarce. Drachm

BACTRIA. Horseman to right; rev. a bull. Fair. Rare. Drachm

PARTHIA. Sapir II. Bust to right; rev. Fire altar, pierced. Drachm

——— Varahran II. Bust to right; rev., as above, pierced in two places. Rubbed. Drachm

——— Chosroes 1. Bust to right within a wreath; rev. as above. Fair. Drachm

ROMAN SILVER.

Denarii.

MARC ANTONY. Obv. Three military standards; rev. a galley. Fair

AUGUSTUS. Laureated head to r.; rev. Caius and Lucius each holding a lance and shield. Very good

AUGUSTUS. Similar

TIBERIUS. Head to right; rev. seated female holding a spear and flower. (The so-called Tribute Penny.) Good; scarce

VITELLIUS. Head to right; revs. different. *Plated.* Poor 2 pcs

VESPASIAN. Head to right; rev. Victory seated. Very good

TITUS. Head laureated to r; rev. a tripod. Good; scarce

DOMITIAN. Head to right; rev. Minerva standing. Good

NERVA. Head to right; rev. Liberty standing. Very fair; scarce

TROJAN. Head to r. laureate; rev. DACIA CAPTA. Female seated on armor. Fair

HADRIAN. Head to r.; rev. Seated victory. Good 2 pcs

16 681 ANTONIUS PIUS and Faustina.   Heads to right; revs. a
temple and Venus standing.   Fair   2 pcs

18 682 LUCIUS VERUS and Lucilla.   Heads to right; revs. Abund-
ance and Venus standing.   Very good   2 pcs

10 683 CRISPINA and Sept. Severus.   Heads to right; revs. an
armed warrior and Venus.   Barely fair   2 pcs

18 684 CARACALLA and Geta.   Heads to right; revs. Two stand-
. ing figures.   Fine pair   2 pcs

9 685 JULIA SOEMIAS.   Busts to r.; revs. Victory.   Poor   2 pcs

/ 55 686 ~~CONSTANS~~.   Bust to right with beaded fillet; rev. Ins.
within a wreath,   Very good

55 687 JULIA (Consular denarius).   Obv. CAESAR, an elephant;
rev. Sacrificial instruments.   Fine; scarce

NOTE. The Denarii that follow are debased silver or *billon*.   All
have heads to the right and condition from fine to fair.

16 688 ETRUSCILLA, Salonina, Otacillia.   Fine   3 pcs

11 689 GORDIANUS PIUS III.   Fine and fair   2 pcs

15 690 PHILIPPUS, Trajanus Decius.   Fine   2 pcs

16 691 POSTUMUS, Trebonianus Gallus.   Fine   2 pcs

12 692 PHILIPPUS.   Very good   2 pcs

11 693 GALLIENUS.   Gallus and Vibius.   Very good   3 pcs

MISCELLANEOUS.

Copper

32 694 ENGLAND.   *Edelred Rex*.   ~~Silver~~ scættæ.   Fine and scarce

21 695 ——— Elizabeth.   Shilling; m.m. Double Cross.   Rubbed

11 696 RUSSIA and South America.   2 silver coins.   Value about
15 cents   2 pcs

55 697 Medal of Louis XIV.   Bust to l.   Hair in long curls ; rev.
View of the country.   A very large sunflower in the
right foreground.   Full-faced sun in sky, "Au gre de mon
soleil."   Very fine.   Bronze.   S. 39

1¾ 698 Miscellaneous lot of Coppers, including 2 Admiral Vernon
Medals.   Very ordinary lot   27 pcs

FOREIGN COPPER COINS.

80 699 Liberia, 1862.   Cent.   Legend incused.   Uncirculated.   Proof
surface

17 700 Roumania, 1879.   5 Para.   Uncirculated.   Red

30 701 Papal States, 1868. 4 Soldi. Uncirculated. Red

3 702 France, 1790. Monneron Cinq-Solo. Uncirculated. 2 or 3 scratches on rev.

12 703 Hawaii, Kamehameha III., 1847. Hapa Hanero. Good
2 pcs

704 Guernesey. 8, 4, 2, and 1 Doubles. Scarce as a set. Good. The 2 doubles abused
4 pcs

6 705 Guernesey. 4 Doubles (2), Sarawak Cent, 1863, and Cent of Republic of Haiti, 1863 (2). Good.

18 706 Ionian Islands, 1819, '20· Penny, Farthing, and Half do. Very fair
3 pcs

9 707 Sweden. Baron Goertz Dalers. 7 varieties and one duplicate. Very good
8 pcs

6 708 England. Wine Farthing. " Good wine needs no bush." Very good

70 709 Ceylon, 1802. Elephant ; rev. 192 etc. Farthing size. Brass proof

710 Liverpool. Kettlewell's card. Brass. Uncirculated. Farthing size

3 711 France. 10, 5, and 2 Centimes. Uncirculated
3 pcs

2 712 Germany, Sweden, &c. 1 Kreutzer, 1 and 2 Ore, 1 Pfenning and 1 Rin. Uncirculated. Red
9 pcs

42 713 Siberia, Catherine II. 10 Kopecs. Arms supported by Foxes. Very good

12 714 Siberia, Catherine II. 2 Kopecs. Same type. Good

1 715 Austria. 4 Kreutzers (3), uncirculated, and German War Medal. Good
4 pcs

18 716 Cuba. 10, 5 and 2½ Centavos. Patterns. Proofs. Scarce
3 pcs

10 717 Brazil. 100 Reis. Nickel (2) and 3 Coppers of Central America
5 pcs

10 718 Liberia Cent and Coventry Half-Penny. Lady Godiva. Fair
2 pcs

1 719 Canada, Nova Scotia and New Brunswick Pennies. Varieties. Good
6 pcs

1½ 720 Canada (5), New Brunswick (2), Prince Edward's Island, and Nova Scotia (8), Half-Penny Tokens. Good lot. Some scarce
16 pcs

12 721 Sumatra Cent (or Dime). Uncirculated
3 pcs

3 7 722 Sumatra. Dollar and Quarter Dollar size in copper. Good
2 pcs

1/2 723 China. Cash, or as some one has called them, "Pirate Money of Siam." Good
100 pcs

1/2 724 Another lot
100 pcs

1 6 725 Another lot
100 pcs

1 6 726 Another lot
100 pcs

1/2 727 Another lot
100 pcs

1 6 728 Another lot
90 pcs

3 729 Lot of foreign Coppers, mostly Penny and Two-Penny size of England, Spain, France, etc., etc. Very good; desirable lot
44 pcs

1 3/4 730 Another lot, Half-Penny to Farthing size, various countries. Good lot. 2 pierced
155 pcs

3 1/2 731 Moorish Coins. Good lot
12 pcs

1 0 732 Ancient. First Brass of Marcus Aurelius, Balbinus, and Second Brass of Nero, Germanicus, etc. Barely fair and good
7 pcs

6 733 Greek Colonials of Probus, etc. Fine lot
11 pcs

8 734 Small brass box, containing the little birth Medals of the Royal Family of England
7 pcs

U. S. CENTS, HALF-CENTS, AND COLONIALS, &c.

800 735 1793 Wreath. Stars and bars on edge. Even dark color. Slight corrosion on rev. A slight break in rev. die runs from stem of wreath through c and a of America to the edge. Nearly uncirculated, and a very desirable cent. Rare in this condition

3 10 736 1793 Wreath. Same type. The leaves under bust spread. Perfect die. Good for date

2 60 737 1793 Chain. Dark color. Weakly struck. Fair

1 2 738 1793 Liberty cap. Broken die. Very poor. Date and rev. not visible

2 2 739 1793 Wreath Cent. Beautiful electrotype of a very fine cent

2 6 740 1793 Chain light brown color. A very fine electrotype.

5 1/2 741 1795, '6 (2 varieties), '7 (2), '8 (6), 1800 (3), '1 (3), '2 (3). Fair
20 pcs

44 742 1796 Liberty cap and fillet head.   Very fair   2 pcs

57 743 1798 Light brown color.   Nearly uncirculated

33 744 1799 Light brown color.   Good ; altered date

4½ 745 1800, '3 (5), '5, '6 (3), '7, '8 (2), '10 (2), '11, '12 (3), '13 (3), '14
(2).   Fair, 5 of them poor   24 pcs

55 746 1804 Very poor and pierced

50 747 1810 Dark brown color.   Fine

4/ 748 1816 Die broken on edge.   Uncirculated.   Red

110 749 1817 15 stars.   Beautiful orange-red color, polished surface ; has been doctored.   A very beautiful and desirable
cent.   Scarce.

2½ 750 1816 (2), '17 (2), '18 (2), '19, '20, '22, '23 (4), '24, '25 (2), '26,
'28 (3), '29, '30, '31, '32 (2).   Fair   25 pcs

210 751 1825 Light steel-brown color.   Uncirculated

47 752 1826   Fine

2 753 1833 (3), ('34, '36, '37, '38 (3), '39, '40 (3), '41 (2), '42 (2), '43
(4), '44 (4).   Fair to good   25 pcs

40 754 1837 Olive-brown color.   Uncirculated

22 755 1839 Silly and booby heads.   Good   2 pcs

2¾ 756 1838, '45 (4), '46 (2), '47 (3), '48 (2), '49 (2), '50 (2), '51,
'52, '53, '54 (4), '55 (6), '56 (2), '57 (2).   Good to fine.
33 pcs

7 757 1846, '47, '48, '54 (3), '55 (2).   Very fine and uncirculated.
8 pcs

12 758 1855 Straight date.   Uncirculated.   Golden

20 759 1855 Another.   Uncirculated.   Golden

28 760 1857 Small date.   Good and very good   2 pcs

5 761 Half Cents.   1800, '3, '4, '5, '7, '8, '9, '11, '25, '26 (pierced),
'28, '29, '33, '34.   Very fair   14 pcs

21 762 Cent of 1853.   Flattened out thin, and a silver 3-cent piece
pressed into the rev.   The job performed at the Centennial.   Curious.   Unique   Size 24

1 763 Nickel Cents.   1857 (2), '58 (4), '59, '60, '62, '63 (2), '64.
Fine   12 pcs

1 764 Bronze Cents.   1864 (2), '65, '67, '68 (2), '69, '70, '71,
'73, '74, '75, '76, '78, '79, '80 (3), '81 (12), '82 (8), '83, '84.
Very good to fine and uncirculated.   40 pcs

½ 765 Rebellion Tokens, or " Copperheads."   Good lot   83 pcs

6 5 766 Vermont Cent. 1786. "Vermontensium." 9 trees. Nearly
  fine

2 / 767 New Jersey. 1787 and 1788. George III.; rev. Inde et
  lib. Very good   Lead   2 pcs

7 768 New York. Libernatus Libertatem Defendo. Very fine
  electrotype

2 769 Washington large and small eagle Cent, 1791, and Liberty
  and Security, Two-Pence. Good. Electrotypes 3 pcs

1/4 770 Store Cards. Size of the old copper cent, and proofs in copper, brass, and w. m.   20 pcs

2/4 771 Another lot. Copper, brass, white metal, and nickel. Uncirculated and proof   15 pcs

1/2 772 Another lot. Same metals. Same   14 pcs

5 773 Hotel Brighton, Coney Island, Cheeks, 50, 25, 10 and 5 cents.
  Brass proof. Beautiful set   4 pcs

10 774 W. A. Thomson, Buffalo. Teapot; rev. anvil. Cop.; good;
  scarce   Size 21

2 775 S. L. Wilkins, Lowell. Rev. Lafayette. Very good

10 776 John J. Adams, 11 Main St., Taunton. Rev. a boar running. Fine

18 777 Wood's Minstrels' Card, 1857. Silver proof Size 6

18 778 Washington Temperance Benevolent Soc. Head; rev.
  "We serve," etc. Silver; pierced   Size 13

17 779 M. L. Marshall's Variety Store, Oswego. Silver proof
           Size 18

5 780 H. G. Sampson's Store Card. W. m. proof Size 27

1/2 781 Store Cards. V. Kinsey, Cinn.; F. C. Key & Sons, Phila.,
  &c., in cop., br., and w. m. Unc. and proofs 10 pcs

2 782 Politicals. U. S. Grant. Varieties. Cop. br. and w. m.
  proof. Size 13 and 17   6 pcs

6 783 Politicals. Washington. Cop., br., w. m., nickel and
  bronze proofs. Size 15 to 22.   7 pcs

3/2 784 Politicals. Greeley (3), Grant (2), Seymour (2), McClellan (2), Hayes (2). Cop., br. and w. m. proof. Size 14
  to 18   11 pcs

8 785 Lincoln; rev. ins. in 9 lines. Washington, the California
  Centennial Medal. White metal proofs. Size 26. 2 pcs

5 786 Washington Perpetual Calendar. Fine. Copper Size 21

2 787 Penn. State Agricultural Fair. Brass proof Size 16

Centennial Medals, Coat-of-Arms. Various reverses. W.
m. proof. Size 15   8 pcs
Another set. Liberty bell. Same   8 pcs
Another set. Continental soldier. Same   8 pcs
Another set. Head of Liberty. Same, and one with State
House   9 pcs

A FEW MEDALS AND SILVER COINS.

Abraham Lincoln. Head to l. "Dé die par la Democratie
Française a Lincoln President Deux fois elu des Etats
Unis"; rev. Tomb with long inscription in French. An
angel with anchor to l.; slaves to r. In high relief.
A very beautiful and rare Medal. Dies by *Magniadas*.
Obv. slightly injured by corrosion. Bronze   Size 53
Washington; rev. To the Japanese Embassy from Bailey
& Co. Bronze proof   Size 34
Washington Masonic Medal; rev. Implements. Bronze.
Very fine   Size 33
Centennial Award Medal. Bronze. Very fine   Size 34
H. G. Sampson's Card. Copper proof. Scarce in copper
Size 27
Medal struck on the completion of the railroad to Berlin,
1844. Bronze proof   Size 29
Gen. Zachary Taylor. Bust; rev. ins. in 10 lines. Dies
by *C. C. Wright*. Very fine   Size 37
New York Free Academy Medal. Bust of Liberty; rev.
ins. in 12 lines. Considerably nicked. Bronze Size 38
Washington. "Siege of Boston" Medal. Silver proof
Size 20
Washington. Four varieties in c., b., w. m. And Stephen
A. Douglas. Cop. Fine   5 pcs
Phallic Medal. A *very free* subject, equal to any of the
Pompeian frescoes. Cast in iron. No rev. Very rare
Size 55
Very similar   Size 55
1862 Pattern 10 Dollars in copper. Uncirculated
Pattern 2½ Dollars in copper. Uncirculated
1795 Half-Dollar. Very fair

13 807 1879 Quarter and Dime. 1829, '30 Half-Dime. Uncirculated   4 pcs

4 808 1883 5 Cents, figure 5 and V; and 3 Cents. Nickel. Proofs
     3 pcs

6 809 Lot of Silver, English, Chinese, &c. Face value about 65
cents   10 pcs

20 810 Bracteates. Large and very fine. Rare. Size 20   8 pcs

21 811 Piece of the first Atlantic Cable. Length, 4 inches

23 812 Another piece, same size

140 813 Powerful Magnifying Glass on tripod, brass mountings.
Very powerful lens. Diam., 1¾ inches

POSTAGE STAMPS, ETC.

16.00 814 ~~Collection~~ of stamps including all countries; ~~a full line U.
S. department stamps~~, many very rare; a large and inter-
esting assortment, all in envelopes properly marked
Dealers lot of numerous duplicates   2,900 pcs

lot 2.60 815 Lot of miscellaneous stamps; a great variety   2,200 pcs

10 816 Chinese bank bill for $10, gold, redeemable on presentation
at the Royal (Washy Washy) Bank, Canton. Fine.
Rare *Bill of exchange*

2½ 817 Lot of old play books, a great variety, mostly published in
New York at the beginning of this century. 12mo,
unbound   53 pcs

CONFEDERATE NOTES.

Arranged by Hazeltine's List.

JULY 25, 1861.

9 818 $100. Two females in centre, C. 7

4 819 $50. Head of Washington in centre, B. & C. 8   2 pcs

4 820 $20. Ship in centre. 9

10 821 $10. Female, eagle and Confederate flag in centre. 11

2 822 $10. Same, mended. 11   11 pcs

80 823 $5. Female, eagle and 5 in centre. ~~New and clean.~~ Rare.
12

2 824 $5. Same. Torn. Rare. 12

2.50 825 $5. FIVE across left end; "Confederate States of Amer-
ica" in blue on back. Fine; very rare. 13
torn on one end

September 2, 1861.

8 826 $100. Men loading wagon. 14

2 827 $50. Seated figure with money chests. 16

6 828 $50. Head of Davis in centre. 19

125 829 $20. Three females in centre. Green note. Rare. 24

2 830 $10. Negro picking cotton in centre. 30

55 831 $10. Group of Indians in centre, female holding X on right. Partly red. Very fine and rare. 34

110 832 $10. Wagon loaded in centre, Xs and ten red. Very fine. Rare. 35

2 833 $10. Two females and urn. 36 and 37   10 pcs

5 834 $10. Head of R. M. T. Hunter; red Xs coarsely figured

130 835 $10. Female, shield and eagle in upper left corner; small piece gone from upper left corner. Fine ; very rare. 41

37 836 $5. Group of Indians in centre, statue of Washington on right; partly red. Very fine and rare. 42

105 837 $5. Machinist on right, vignette of boy on left; partly red. Very fine ; very rare. 44

100 838 $5. Same

2 839 $10. Sept. 2, 1862, female seated on barrel. 67   5 pcs

2 840 H. Nos. 21, 25, 31, 36, 38, 53, 67   7 pcs

1862.

7 841 $100. Head of Mrs. Davis in centre. New. 68

9 842 $50. Head of Davis in centre. New. 69

April 6, 1863.

2 843 $50. Head of Davis in centre. New. 87

2 844 $20. Capitol at Nashville. New. 91

6 845 $10. Capitol at Montgomery. New. 93

8 846 $5. Capitol at Richmond. New. 97

5 847 $5. Same design. New. 98   5 pcs

2 848 $1. Head of C. C. Clay. New. 109

2 849 50 Cents. Vignette of Davis. New. 112   10 pcs

February 17, 1864.

18 850 $100. Head of Mrs. Davis. Small size note. Rare. 115

20 851 $100. Same   5 pcs

2 852 $20. XI Series. New. Scarce. 117
2 853 $5. Capitol at Richmond. 119   10 pcs
3½ 854 $2. Head of Benjamin. New. 120   10 pcs
3½ 855 $1. Head of C. C. Clay in centre. New. 134   10 pcs
    NOTE.—None of the above notes are cancelled.

SILVER CROWNS OF BRUNSWICK AND LUNE-BURG.

3 6 0 856 1524 Busts of Henry and Ehrick ; rev. Arms, surmounted
        by a wild man. Fine; rare
1 6 0 857 1572 Julius. Wild man with tree and candle, 15—72; rev.
        Arms, two wild men as *supporters*. Good; scarce.
2 4 0 858 1586 Julius. *Spectacle Crown*. Wild man with tree, candle,
        skull, hour-glass and spectacles to l., $^{15-86}_{14-\text{JUNI}}$; rev. Arms
        surmounted by three crests. Fine; scarce
2 4 0 859 1588 Julius. *Spectacle Crown*. Wild man with tree and
        horse to l., hour-glass, spectacles, &c., to r.; rev. Arms.
        Fine; scarce
8 0 860 1588 Julius. *Spectacle Half-Crown*. Same type. Good;
        very rare
2 7 0 861 1589 Julius. Mortuary Crown. Bust to waist in armor,
        with battle-axe; rev. Wild man with tree, hour-glass and
        spectacles leaning on a tablet with ins. in 5 lines. Fine;
        rare
2 2 5 862 1596 Philip. Mortuary Crown. " Obiit . IIII . April . Anno .
        M . D . XCVI . vixit . Ann . LXII . Mens . XI."; rev. Arms sur-
        mounted by two crests. Fine; very rare
1 8 0 863 1597 Henry Julius. Bust. to l.; rev. Arms. Very good
1 7 5 864 1597 Henry Julius. *Truth Crown*. Christ standing on two
        prostrate figures. "Veritas" above ins. in field, eleven
        shields surrounding; rev. Inscription. Fine
1 2 5 865 1597 Henry Julius. *Truth Crown*. A variety. Very good
1 4 0 866 1598 Henry Julius. *Truth Crown*. Similar type. Very
        good; rare
1 5 0 867 1599 Henry Julius. *Pelican Crown*. Pelican feeding her
        young. "Pro Aris et Focis" and four bunches of arrows
        surrounding; rev. Arms, wild man to r. Very good;
        scarce

2 0 5 868 1602 Henry Julius. Mortuary Crown of his mother Hedwig. Arms, wild man to r. ; rev. "D. M. Illso. Princ. D. N. Hedwigi," etc., in eleven lines. Fine; rare

1 6 0 869 1604 Henry Julius. Arms surmounted by five crests; rev. Wild man and thick branchless tree. Very good

1 5 5 870 1608 Henry Julius. Rev. Wild man and slim tree with one small branch. Very good

1 7 0 871 1608 Henry Julius. Same type, but a variety. Fine

4 2 872 1610 Henry Julius. Arms, no crests; rev. Wild man and tree. ¼ Crown. Very fair

1 5 5 873 1611 Henry Julius. Arms, five crests; rev. Wild man and tree. Very good

4 2 874 1611 Henry Julius. Wild man. ¼ Crown. Very good

1 5 0 875 1613 Henry Julius. Mortuary Crown. Arms, no crests; rev. Ins. in 9 lines. Fine; rare

1 6 5 876 1614 Fr. Ulric. Arms, five crests; rev. Wild man and tree with one branch. Very good

1 7 0 877 1615 Fr. Ulric. Rev. Wild man and tree with *four* branches. Very good. Scarce

1 6 0 878 1616 Fr. Ulric. Rev. Wild man and branchless tree. Very fine

1 5 0 879 1616 Fr. Ulric. Similar, but a marked variety. Very good

1 6 5 880 1622 Fr. Ulric. Rev. A very peculiar wild man with long pointed beard and mustache, with branchless tree. s. a. in monogram counterstamped between wild man's feet. Very good

3 3 5 881 1622 Christian. "Gottes Freundt Derpeaffen Feindt;" rev. A mailed arm, holding a sword, issuing from clouds; obv. die broken. ~~Very~~ fine and exceedingly rare

1 5 5 882 1624 Fred. Ulric; rev. Wild man with tree. Very good

1 4 5 883 1624 William. Bust in Armor to r.; rev. Arms. Very fine; rare

1 1 5 884 1625 Christian. Bust to r.; rev. Arms. Fine

1 5 0 885 1626 Fr. Ulric. Arms; rev. Wild man and tree with one short twig. Good

1 5 0 886 1626 Fr. Ulric. Similar, but a marked variety. Very good

/30 887 1627 Christian. Bust to r. in rich robes ; rev. Arms. Very
fine

/55 888 1627 Fr. Ulric. Arms; rev. Wild man and tree with one
twig. Good

/55 889 1628 Fr. Ulric; rev. Wild man and tree. . Fine

/65 890 1629 Fr. Ulric; rev. Wild man and branchless tree. Fine

/50 891 1630 Fr. Ulric; rev. Wild man. Very good

/60 892 1633 Christian. Mortuary Crown; arms; rev. Ins. in ten
lines. Very fine; very rare

/70 893 1637 Augustus; rev. Wild man with fir tree ; two fir trees
in back ground. Very good; scarce

/25 894 1639 George. Bust to waist in rich robes to l. with sceptre;
rev. Arms. Very fine

/15 895 1643 Frederick. Bust to r.; rev. Arms. Very fine

/15 896 1643 Augustus. Bust to the waist with sceptre; rev. Arms.
Very good

/30 897 1651 Augustus. Arms; rev., Wild man. Good

/40 898 1652 Augustus ; rev. Wild man and tree. Very fair.
Scarce

/25 899 1653 Augustus. Bust ¾ face to l.; rev. Arms. Very good;
scarce

55 900 1655 Augustus. ¼ crown; arms; rev. Wild man and tree.
Fine; rare

/65 901 1656 Augustus. Arms; rev. Wild man with fir tree across
his knees. Very good; scarce

/75 902 1658 Augustus. Same type. Very fine; scarce

/50 903 1658 Augustus; rev. Wild man with fir tree to r. Very
good

/80 904 1658 Augustus. Bust nearly front face, within a wreath;
ins. on scroll; rev. Arms within a wreath; ins. on scroll.
Very fine; rare

/45 905 1658 George William. Arms; rev. Wild man facing to r.,
tree to l. Fine; rare

/35 906 1659 George William; rev. Wild man with tree to l. Very
good; scarce

/20 907 1660 Augustus. Same type as lot 901. Good. Dark.
Scarce

205 908 1662 Charles Ludwig; rev. Wild man with legs crossed,
tree to r. Fine; rare

145⁻ 909 1665 George William; rev. Wild man with tree to l. Very good; scarce

150 910 1665 Augustus. Same type. Fine; rare

160 911 1666 Augustus; rev. Wild man and fir tree to r. Fine; scarce

160 912 1666 Augustus. *Birthday Crown;* Bust, nearly front face; Victory above, with trumpet and wreath; rev. Arms *supported* by two wild men. Fine; scarce

60 913 1666 Augustus. Mortuary ½ Crown; ins. in eleven lines within circle of ins.; rev. Tree, inscription surrounding. Very broad. Fine; rare   Size 29

40 914 1666 Augustus. Mortuary ¼ Crown; same type. Very broad. Fine; rare   Size 23

145⁻ 915 1687 Rudolph Augustus and Anthony Ulric. Arms; rev. *Two* wild men with crossed trees. Very fine

400 916 1672 Medal Double Crown. Memorial Medal of the Siege of Groningen; Arms of the City in frame, surmounted by Victory and trophy of arms, flags, etc.; "Curatores academia Groningæ et Ommelandia;" rev. "In memoriam obsidionis et liberationis Groningæ," etc. Very fine; rare   Size 31

200 917 Medal of Philip IV. of France (Philip le Bel). Bust to r., in rich robes, head crowned and chain net protecting back of head; rev. Long ins. in 17 lines. Very beautiful
                     Size 33

Passed 918 Syracuse. Medallion or DECADRACHM. Small type. Beautiful head of Proserpine to l., with wreath of sedge grass, four dolphins surrounding, shell back of head; rev Quadriga to l. Victory crowning the driver. Trophy of arms in exergue. Somewhat defaced, but still in very good condition for this extremely rare coin. Guaranteed genuine. Limited at $125.00

CONFEDERATE MONEY.
All uncancelled, unless otherwise specified.

1861 ISSUE. WRITTEN DATES.

450 919 $100. Montgomery. Series A. 892. Train of cars to right in centre. Printed by Nat. Bk. Note Co. Uncirculated. Very rare. H. No. 3

363 920 $50. Montgomery. Series A. 922. Negroes hoeing cotton in centre. Uncirculated. Rare. H. No. 5

JULY 25, 1861.

6 921 $100. Two females in centre. Uncirculated. Letter C. H. 7

2 922 $20. Ship under full sail in centre. Uncirculated. H. 9

55 923 $10. Female leaning on shield bearing Confederate flag with 11 stars. Letter A. Fine; rare. H. 11

75 924 $5. Female leaning on a figure 5 in centre. Letter Bb. Very good; rare. H. 12

SEPT. 2, 1861.

8 925 $100. Men loading wagon with bales of cotton in centre. Sailor in lower left corner. Uncirculated. H. No. 15

75 926 $50. Train of cars in centre. Female figures in r. and l. corners. Cancelled by cut. Very fine; very rare. H. 18

5 927 $20. Head of Stephens in lower left hand corner. Seated female. Cupid and bee-hive in centre. H. No. 21 and H. 25 (2). Fine.   3 pcs

25 928 $20. Three females in centre. Figure of Liberty to l. Green note. Cancelled by cut. Fine; rare. H. 24

16 929 $20. Kneeling female. Globe and ship in centre. Blacksmith in lower r. and Indian in lower l. corner. Partly red. Letter A. Cancelled by cut. Fine; very rare

16 930 $20. Same

40 931 $20. Same

26 932 $20. Same

8 933 $10. Head of Hunter in lower left corner. Bust of Duncan's child in lower r. corner. Letter J. and K. Fine and scarce. H. 32   2 pcs

65 934 $10. Group of Indians in centre. Indian female with X to r. Seated female with trident to l. Partly red. Very fine. Letter A. Rare. H. 34

60 935 $10. Same type. Letter B. Cancelled by cut. Very fine; rare. H. No. 34

115 936 $10. Wagon with cotton in centre. Head of Postmaster Olden in lower left corner. Man in cornfield in lower r. corner. Partly red. Fine; very rare. H. No. 35

6 937 $10. Female leaning on anchor. Letters X and Y. Very good. H. No. 39   2 pcs

1 938 $10. Same. Cancelled by cut. Letters W. X. and Z. Very good   4 pcs

8 939 $10. Negroes picking cotton in centre. Letter A. Very good. H. No. 30.—And Gen. Marion offering sweet potatoe breakfast. Good. H. No. 31   2 pcs

2 940 $10. Two females with urn in upper left corner. Letters A. 13 and 15. H. No. 36. Fine   2 pcs

105 941 $5. Machinist seated in lower r. corner. Letter A. Very good. H. No. 44. Rare

22 942 $5. Same. Cancelled by cut

18 943 $5. Same as last

18 944 $5. Same as last

15 945 $5. Same, letter B. and another. A piece torn out. Both cancelled   2 pcs

85 946 $5. Group of females in centre. "Five" and 5 in red. Letter A. H. No. 42

90 947 $5. Same

55 948 $5. Negroes loading cotton in lower left corner. Indian in upper right corner. Letters Ab good. Cancelled by cut. H. No. 43. Very rare

2 949 $5. Sailor seated by bales of cotton in centre. Letters B and 8. Very good. H. No. 45   3 pcs

6 950 $5. Female seated on cotton bales. Sailor in lower left corner. A 9 and 10. H. No. 51   2 pcs

10 951 $5. Head of Meninger in centre. Figure of Minerva in upper r. corner. Similar to H. No. 50. No green on note. Series I. Very fine; rare

DECEMBER 2, 1862.

10 952 $100. Head of Mrs. Davis in centre. H. No. 68. Fine.

2 953 $100. Negroes hoeing cotton in centre, 1862 Int. note. Train of cars in centre. $100 (2). Very good lot. H. No. 55 and 56   3 pcs

4 954 $50. Head of Davis in centre. Green note. H. No. 69.— And Cap. at Richmond. $5 note. Blue back. H. No. 80. Fine   2 pcs

10 955 $100. Head of Mrs. Davis ; and $50, head of Jeff. Davis ;
and Capitol at Richmond ; $20 series of April 3, 1883.
H. No. 86, 87 and 97; and $100 series, Feb. 17, 1864,
$100 head of Mrs. Davis in centre, H. No. 114. Fine lot.
4 pcs

MISCELLANEOUS CENTS, Etc.

7 956 Large coppers of Brazil and Portugal, mostly counterstamped 10 pcs

1/4 957 Penny, Half-Pennies (16) and Farthings (5) of Victoria.
Good to uncirculated 22 pcs

1/4 958 Halfpenny tokens of Canada, Prince Edward's Island, Halifax, etc. Good 12 pcs

1/2 959 English, French, Turkish, German, South American, etc.
coppers from Penny to Farthing size. Good lot 100 pcs

12 960 1795. Thin die. 1797, '98· Fair and good 3 pcs

10 961 1800, '1, '2, '3· Ordinary 4 pcs

22 962 1802. Light brown color. Very good

JJ0 963 1809. Light brown color. *Very fine.* Nearly uncirculated impression ; traces of the red still showing. Rare
in this condition *Electrotype*

10 964 1807, '12· Ordinary 2 pcs

10 965 1810, '14· Very fair 2 pcs

10 966 1812, '13· Fair 2 pcs

10 967 1819. Perfect die. Very fine 2 pcs

12 968 1821, '22· Very good 2 pcs

20 969 1823. Ordinary

5 970 1825, '26, '27· The 1827 counterstamped J. W. Carr. Ordinary 3 pcs

2 971 1830, '33, '34, '37· Very good and fine 4 pcs

3 972 1837, '38· Fine 2 pcs

2 973 1840, '42· Good 3 pcs

6 974 1843. Dark steel color. ~~Fine~~ *Stool bleached*

2 975 1845, '46, '47· Fine 3 pcs

20 976 1845, rev. 1846. Double head Cent. Very handy for
gamesters. Ordinary

3 977 1847, '48, '49· Fine. The figure 4 of the '47 altered to a 1,
thus making an 1817 cent out of it 3 pcs

2-978 1851 Very good. A peculiar mark on the check of one. 2 pcs
9 979 1852 Uncirculated. Golden
20 980 1854 Uncirculated. Golden
5 981 1855 Straight fives. Very good 2 pcs
1 2 982 1857 Large and small date. The large date cleaned. Very good 2 pcs
28 983 1795 Half-Cent. Thin die. Fair
9 984 1804, '5, '6, '9, '11, '28, '32 and '35 Half-Cents. Fair and good 8 pcs
1 2 985 1853 Half-Cent. ~~Uncirculated~~
40 986 1837 Half-Cent worth of pure copper. Good
1 987 Lot of Cents. Various dates. Fair and good 60 pcs
3/4 988 Lot of Copperheads. Varieties. Good lot. Good to uncirculated 100 pcs
2-989 Card. Containing one dozen celluloid pins bearing heads of Cleveland and Hendricks. Various colors. Size 23 12 pcs
2 990 Similar lot. Heads of Blaine and Logan 12 pcs
9 991 The Vermont Journal and Universal Advertiser for Aug. 10, 17 and 24, 1790. One small piece gone from one number 3 pcs

AMERICAN SILVER.

DOLLARS.

1 40 992 1795 Flowing hair. Head of 1794. 13 berries on wreath. Very little rubbed. Fine
1 35 993 1795 Flowing hair. Different head. Smaller stars. Fine. Not much rubbed. 17 berries on wreath
1 50 994 1795 Flowing hair. Different head. Lower curl of hair touches star. Close date. 16 berries on wreath. Planchet somewhat haymarked, but a really fine dollar
1 40 995 1795 Flowing hair. Another variety. Lower curl of hair almost touching star. Spread date. 19 berries on wreath. Nearly fine. Somewhat rubbed; rev. fine
1 45 996 1795 Flowing hair. Slight variety. Fine, only slightly rubbed
1 45 997 1795 Flowing hair. Similar. Fine

135 998 1795 Flowing hair. Similar to 993. 17 berries on wreath
Curl touching star. Good. Two nicks on obv.
160 999 1795 Fillet head. Very good
170 1000 1796 Very good
160 1001 1797 7 stars facing. Good; scarce
155 1002 1797 6 stars facing. Good
120 1003 1798 13 stars. Very good ; nearly fine
115 1004 1799 Good
150 1005 1800 Good
130 1006 1801 Good. Scratched
120 1007 1802 Very good. Nicked
130 1008 1802 Over 1. Very good
140 1009 1803 Good
145 1010 1865 Brilliant proof
155 1011 1866 Brilliant proof

HALF DOLLARS.

50 1012 1807 Very good
55 1013 1807 Good
55 1014 1811 Very fine .
55 1015 1817 Fine
55 1016 1828 Uncirculated and brilliant
55 1017 1829 ~~Uncirculated and brilliant~~
50 1018 1830 Very fine
50 1019 1834 Large date. Fine
50 1020 1834 Small date. Uncirculated, weak impression
180 1021 1836 Reeded edge. Very good ; scarce
240 1022 1852 Fine. Phila. mint. Scarce
75 1023 1862 Brilliant proof
75 1024 1866 Brilliant proof
60 1025 1867 Proof. Slightly tarnished
65 1026 1868 Proof. Slightly tarnished
75 1027 1869 Brilliant proof
80 1028 1870 Brilliant proof
60 1029 1875 Scratched proof

QUARTER DOLLARS.

25 1030 1818 Good
30 1031 1819 Good

2 5 1032 1831 Very fine
2 5 1033 1834 Good
3 6 1034 1836 Fine
2 5 1035 1856 Fine
2 5 1036 1861 Fine
2 5 1037 1865 Uncirculated
2 5 1038 1868 Uncirculated and scarce
3 0 1039 1869 ~~Uncirculated~~ and scarce
3 1 1040 1871 Uncirculated
2 5 1041 1873 With arrows. Uncirculated
3 0 1042 1878 Proof
3 0 1043 1879 Brilliant proof
3 0 1044 1880 ~~Proof~~
3 0 1045 1880 ~~Proof~~

DIMES.

1046 1829 Good
1047 1830 Good
1048 1832 Very good
1049 1834 Fine
/0 1050 1835 Very good
1051 1845 Fine
1052 1853 With arrows. Fine
1053 1856 O Mint. Very good
1054 1858 Fine
2 0 1055 1883 Base money set. 3 varieties of 5, 3 and 1. Brilliant
proofs   5 pcs
2 0 1056 1883 Another set. Brilliant proofs   5 pcs
6 00 1057 1879 Stella, or Four Dollar Pattern piece. Proof. Gold.
Scarce
/90 1058 1879 Goloid Metric Pattern Dollar. Brilliant proof.
Scarce
/90 1059 1879 Metric Dollar. Pattern. Brilliant proof. Scarce

U. S. CENTS, &c.

6/2 1060 1794 to '98, 1800 to '3, '5 to '8, '10, '12, '14 to '23. Very fair and good   25 pcs

4 1061 1794, '98, 1803, '5, '12, '14, '16, '17 (both varieties) '18 to '21. Fair to good   13 pcs

2 1062 1794, '5 (2), '6 (2), '7 (2), '8 (5), 1800 (4), '1 (4), '2 (5), '3 (8), '5 (3, 1 pierced), '6, '7 (3), '8 (2), '10 (2), '12 (3), '14 (5, 1 pierced), '16 (2), '17 (13 stars, 8). Poor to ordinary

      62 pcs

/ 7 1063 1797 Doubly struck. One face being on top of the head, forming a head-dress, resembling the lion skin head-dress. The milling and "Liberty" doubly struck. Very curious cent. Very fair

4√ 1064 1804 One pierced. Very poor   2 pcs

7√ 1065 1809 Somewhat injured by corrosion. Very good for date

2 2 1066 1809, '10, '11. Barely fair   3 pcs

√ 1067 1813, '14, '18, '19, '22, '24, '25, '26, '27, '28. Very good to fine   10 pcs

2 6 1068 1817 13 and 15 Stars. Fine   2 pcs

√√ 1069 1823 Perfect die. Good

/ 1070 1818, '19 (2), '29 to 1856. Good lot   31 pcs

/ 1071 1848 (8), '49 (7), '50 (10), '51 (15), '52 (4), '53 (6). Good

      50 pcs

9 1072 1857 Large and small date. Good   4 pcs

//8 1073 1798, 1802, '3, '16 (5), '18 (10), '19 (7), '20 (7), '22 (8), '23, '24 (7), '25 (6), '26 (16), '27 (10), '28 (9), '29 (7), '30 (7), '31 (21), '32 (13), '33 (17). Ordinary   155 pcs

1074 1834 (12), '35 (11), '36 (8), '37 (34), '38 (37), '39 varieties (16), '40 (14), '41 (6), '42 (14), '43 (21), '44 (17), '45 (27). Ordinary   217 pcs

1075 1846 (39), 1847 (68), 1848 (57), 1849 (38), 1850 (36). Good

      238 pcs

1076 1851 (112), '52 (52), '53 (104), '54 (47), '55 (25), '56 (41), '57 pierced. Good   382 pcs

1077 1857 (2), '58 (2), '59, '60, '61, '62, '63, '64 (Nickel), 1864, '65, '66, '68 (2), '73, '79 (2), '80 (2), '81 (51), '82 (8), '84 (2). Uncirculated   81 pcs

1858, '61, '64 (2), '67, '69, '70, '71, '72 (2), '73, '74, '75, '76, '77 (3), 8 and 2 Cents of various dates (9). Ordinary

27 pcs

5 Cents. Nickel, 1883. Without "Cents." Uncirculated

20 pcs

Half-Cents, 1803, '4, '9, '25, '28 (3), '50, '53 (6), '56. Ordinary

15 pcs

Base Money. Proof sets, 1880 and 1881. 5, 3, 1   6 pcs

Base Money. Proof set, 1882. 5, 3, 1.   2 sets   6 pcs

1836 First steam coinage, and removal of Conn. battle flags. Bronze and copper. Very fine   2 pcs

Coventry Half-Penny. Lady Godiva, 1792 and 1794. Varieties. Fair and good   ·   2 pcs

1783 Washington and Independence Cent. 1837. Millions for defence; rev. head. 1855; rev. "Not one cent but just as good." Ordinary   3 pcs

Lot of Cents. 1810 (5), '14 (2), '17 (8), '18 (20), '19 (13), '20 (4), '22 (18), '24 (17). Fair to good   87 pcs

1818 Connected stars. Uncirculated. Golden. Stained ·

12 pcs

Lot of Cents. 1825 (8), '27 (6), '28 (9), '29 (12), '30 (2), '32 (4), '33 (6), '34 (3), '35 (2), '36, '37 (3), '38 (9). Fair to good   ·   65 pcs

Cents. Varieties. Ordinary   13 pcs

Lot of Cents. 1840 (7), '41 (11), '42 (11), '43 (11), '44 (3), '45 (13), '46 (18). Good   74 pcs

Lot of Cents. 1848 (10), '49 (4), '50 (4), '51 (2), '52, '54 (7), '55 (5), '56 (11). Good   44 pcs

Jewitt, L. Hand-book of English Coins, from the Norman Conquest to present time. With 11 plates in silver and copper. 16mo, cloth, gilt edges. Lond., n. d.

15 Cents Postage Currency. Heads of Grant and Sherman. Autographic Signatures. Red back. Good ; rare

Same. Slightly injured ; nothing gone. Rare

Lot of Priced Catalogues. Priced in lead pencil   26 pcs

Lot of Unpriced Catalogues   75 pcs

Lot of Miscellaneous Numismatic Literature   22 pcs

Lot Literary Matter, including Harper's Young People (54), Vol. V.; Vols. 1, 2 and 3 Our Continent (52); Novels (7); and the Nation, Vols. 35, '36 (14)   127 pcs

1099 Black Walnut Cabinet and Desk Combined.   Total height,
40.00   6 feet 4 in. ; width, 3 feet 11 in. ; depth of desk, 27 in.
      Has 3 drawers and 2 closets, 7 large pigeon-holes, with a
      cylinder front.   The desk proper is surmounted by a Coin
      Cabinet in three sections, each with double doors, and
      containing a total of 42 drawers, 36 of which are 12x15 in.;
      $\frac{7}{8}$, $\frac{5}{8}$ and $\frac{1}{2}$ in. in depth, and 6 are $9\frac{1}{4}$x$10\frac{3}{4}$in., $\frac{5}{8}$ in. in depth.
      Locks to all the doors, &c.   In perfect condition ; made
      to order, and has never been used

1100 Cherry Wood Coin Cabinet.   With glass doors.   2 feet $9\frac{1}{2}$
4.50   in. in height; 17 in. in width; $12\frac{1}{2}$ in. deep.   16 drawers.
      15x10x1 in.   White knobs on drawers

1101 Metallic Coin Box, with stand and brass handle.   Contains
5.00   25 movable trays of suitable depth.   With lock and key.
      Dimensions 12x$9\frac{1}{2}$x$10\frac{1}{2}$ in.

COLLECTIONS

OF

COINS AND MEDALS

And Curiosities of Every Description

CAREFULLY CATALOGUED AND ARRANGED FOR SALES AT AUCTION AT THE LOWEST POSSIBLE RATES, BY

H. G. SAMPSON,

Cor. Broadway and Fulton St.,
NEW YORK.

MR. SAMPSON also represents the following INSURANCE COMPANIES :—

THE PHŒNIX INSURANCE CO., OF ENGLAND.

HAMBURG-BREMEN, OF GERMANY.

WESTCHESTER, OF NEW YORK.

GERMANIA, OF NEWARK.

COMMERCIAL, OF NEW YORK.

He will issue policies at reasonable and satisfactory rates, and pledges himself to use every exertion in his power to secure the confidence of his patrons, and the approbation of all parties concerned.

Reside- —No. 91 Bushwick Avenue, Brooklyn, E. D.